Praise for *Insatiable*

"In this no-holds-barred memoir—which at times takes on the form of letters, haiku, and diary entries—Akira shares her personal experiences working as a celebrated porn actress. . . . [Akira] gives intriguing insight into the industry, particularly the bits about porn stars' private and public lives and her own attempt to maintain a meaningful romantic relationship."   —*Publishers Weekly*

"In her debut book, Akira finds an inimitable voice from the inside in a world where porn is increasingly becoming part of the mainstream."   —Examiner.com

"*Insatiable* is, at turns, laugh-out-loud funny, poignant, and out-rageously politically incorrect. . . . But above all else, it's a brutally honest look at one woman's journey through the adult industry, which Akira says the ultimate culmination of her exhibitionist fantasies."   —Daily Dot

"My biggest takeaway from *Insatiable* is Akira understands the true value of her work to herself and her audience, and what a rarity it is to actually love your job. . . . Akira walked into her life without blinders or expectations and discovered what her true happiness is, and that's enough."   —LitReactor.com

"Akira gives even the most household items . . . an entirely new meaning. Forget all the stuff you thought you knew about porn—truth is, you'll never look at baby wipes, Q-tips, or Ziploc bags the same way again."   —*LA Weekly*

"Asa Akira is the latest addition in a wave of highly raunchy but fiercely unapologetic female porn stars."   —*Globe and Mail*

Insatiable

PORN - A Love Story

Insatiable
PORN - A Love Story

ASA AKIRA

Grove Press
New York

Published simultaneously in Canada
Printed in the United States of America

ISBN 978-0-8021-2349-7
eISBN 978-0-8021-9259-2

Grove Press
an imprint of Grove/Atlantic, Inc.
154 West 14th Street
New York, NY 10011

Distributed by Publishers Group West

www.groveatlantic.com

17 18   10 9 8 7 6 5 4 3

To my parents. But please don't read it.

Contents

Author's Note

I started this book hoping to shed a different light on the industry I love so much. Not to say every day is sunshine and flowers, but I don't feel a healthy, honest voice of someone currently looking from the inside out has been heard.

While writing, the book morphed into something more. I've always questioned why I am the way I am. I had a normal upbringing. My parents are loving, kind, and present. I have no mental disorders. Why am I so sexual? Why do I insist on publicizing my most intimate moments?

I can't say that I've found an answer—but writing this book has oddly brought me to peace with myself. At the end of the day, I do feel my sexual cravings as a woman are normal, and should be accepted as such by society. It's bullshit that a man who fucks a thousand women is considered a badass, while a woman doing the same thing is shunned. I'm not ashamed that I've worked at an S&M dungeon, stripped, escorted, or that I currently have sex for money every day. On the contrary, I'm proud of myself for having the guts to indulge in my desires.

The world has seen every fold of my most private body parts, and yet, I feel this book is my most exposing venture yet. I hope you enjoy.

P.S. Some (but not all) of the names I use in the book have been changed.

1

The Perfect Scene

"Rolling and . . . action."

Bobby was going down on Monica. I stood behind the camera, watching. Narrowing his eyes at me, Bobby buried his face in Monica's pussy as he took his cock out to stroke. It was growing harder by the second, and my pussy grew wetter in unison, as if the two were synced. I watched Monica arch her back every time Bobby sucked on her clit and brought her closer to orgasm.

"Come on, fucking come," I mentally whispered. It would be my cue to join them.

I was playing a hooker today. Bobby and Monica were playing a curious couple who hired me. There's something oddly self-referential about playing a hooker in a porno—I was getting paid to portray a woman who got paid to have sex. And also, of course, to have sex. It's like a Russian dolls of sex workers.

As Monica's body twitched, I walked in front of the camera and cupped my hand over her mouth. I gave her one last chance to gasp for air before clamping down on her face, and rubbed her clit hard as Bobby stuck his dick in her. No matter how aggressively she turned and twisted, I wouldn't let her go, and I wouldn't stop rubbing. She continued orgasming for another ten seconds, her muffled screams occasionally escaping through the cracks in my fingers, until I let her free to breathe. As she came down from the intensity, I kissed my way up from her knee to her toes, which curled when Bobby hit a good spot with his cock.

Bobby's cock is great for porn. Big, straight, all one color. It was shiny from the juice coming out of Monica's pussy, making it look as if Monica was giving birth to it. I dived down to suck the slime off, and as I put it back inside her pussy, I spit on my finger and slid it slowly into her asshole. She yelled for more and I stuck another one in. I watched Bobby's dick go in and out of her pussy as I slid my fingers in and out of her ass. I could feel the camera over my shoulder, catching a close-up of the mesmerizing motion.

We made her come again, and I pushed Bobby out of the frame as I climbed on top of Monica to kiss her, then farther up her body until my pussy was on her face. She quickly took my cue to eat me out until I came, collapsing onto my back. Aware of the camera closing in on my face, I eye-fucked Bobby's cock and licked my lips. It wasn't hard to portray—I needed dick. I enjoy getting my pussy eaten as much as the next girl, but when there's a cock in the picture, it feels kind of like going to a steak house and ordering the fish.

Like cock-hungry animals, Monica and I took turns riding Bobby's dick for the following three positions. Finally, as Monica pushed her ass back on Bobby, I got down and licked Bobby's ass. The Euro boys like that. Bobby moaned, and I could tell he was close to cumming. I kept licking, until he finally reached around and pulled me away from his ass by my hair. He grabbed Monica by the head as well, and placed us both on our knees in front of him and came on our faces, and in our mouths. With the cum still dripping off my face, Bobby dragged me up by my arm and bent me over the sofa in the back, and fucked me until I reached another orgasm. I dropped to my knees and crawled to Monica. I spit the remaining cum from my mouth to her pussy. Using my knee to push my hand, my fingers stuffed the cum into her. I fucked her like that until she crossed her eyes and lost it one last time. We made out as our hearts slowed down from racing, and the director yelled "Cut!"

Once in a great while, it happens: the Perfect Scene. It's when everyone, both performers and crew, are all completely synced in energy. Every position, every transition flows organically. The performers lose themselves sexually, yet are fully aware of the camera at all times; the penetration is always on display. The lighting is impeccable, no weird shadows or flares. Animalistic, fluids everywhere, sweat, spit, squirt; the energy is at 100 percent the entire thirty-five minutes, with no cuts. Perhaps a crazy position is invented; standing reverse scissors against a spiral staircase.

You recognize it's happening about halfway through, and once the guy releases a healthy pop shot and the scene is finished, the whole team acknowledges it. The excitement in the room is unmistakable, and everyone's voices are at least a pitch higher than before the shoot started.

"Holy shit, great fucking scene!" the director will exclaim.

"I actually got a boner!" jaded cameraman number two will joke.

"That was one of my top ten scenes ever," I'll declare.

It feels something like just having done a first line of coke together, and everyone wants to talk at once and pat each other on the back for their respective role in the production. It's a high, and every scene we shoot, it's that feeling we are chasing.

A porn set is kind of like Vegas: What happens there, stays there. I always try to make as genuine a connection as possible. From the moment I walk on to the set, everything is dedicated to making the scene better. I get there on time. I laugh at all the jokes. I find something about my partner for the day that I like, whether it be sense of humor, muscular arm, musky scent, whatever. I pay attention to what they like, and try to exaggerate that. When we start having sex, I think about the cameras around us, capturing our sex for countless men to watch and jerk off.

At the risk of sounding overly dramatic, almost every time I shoot a sex scene, I fall a little bit in love. It's the only way I can describe it. Not necessarily with my partner, but just in general. With the situation. In love with being watched. In love with being on display. In love with being the center of attention, for those precious thirty-five minutes. Many people say they disconnect themselves when they have porno sex; I'm the opposite. I'm more present than ever. I try to take in everything and let it turn me on more. Rather than numb myself, I take advantage of the situation and take in as much as I can. A producer set this up for me—to have sex with one of the top talents in the world, in front of a camera, giving me this opportunity to turn the world on; why would I remove myself? Why would I try to mentally put myself anywhere but here? I look into my partners' eyes, and try to portray how much I want them. I tell them how much I like the way they fuck me. I show them how desperate I am for them to feel the same.

Then the guy shoots his load, or the girl will cum on my fingers one last time, the camera cuts, we take a shower, collect our checks, and it's on with the rest of the day.

My very first scene, I took a bus from New York's Port Authority station to Gina Lynn's house in an Amish town in Pennsylvania, and worked for a measly five hundred dollars. When I got on that bus, I had a plan. I would do porn for two years, get it out of my system, save money, and open up a yoga studio.

Fast-forward close to six years, and I'm still in the business. I can't imagine leaving right now. I'm still on my "high," and I don't want to come down. Porn has shaped me, is shaping me, into a woman I had always hoped I would be. I've become more confident, more empowered, more sure of myself than I've ever been. It's a job, but I'm happy to do it every day. There's nothing else I'd rather be doing. I wish I could freeze time and live in this moment forever. I know the clock is ticking. I know soon I'll be too old for this business, and it will be my time to move on to something else.

Legendary pornstar Julia Ann, who's been in the business longer than I've probably been fucking, once told me a story I'll never forget.

"I was watching an interview of myself from ten years ago. It was in the behind-the-scenes footage."

"Hmm."

"I turned to my costar, Janine, and told her, 'If I'm still doing porn at thirty, I'm a fuckin' loser!' We laughed."

Julia Ann is forty-four now. She's found success in other ventures. She's celebrated as a makeup artist and runs her own animal rescue business. She probably has more than enough to retire on.

But she hasn't left porn.

In this way, I feel close to her.

2
Hooking

I've hooked twice. Well, technically three times—but twice was with the same guy.

So I don't know if it counts.

The first time, I went with Laila. Fresh out of a long, drain-circler of a relationship, it was as if she had all of a sudden stormed into the escorting business with some kind of a vengeance. She even did the whole personal phone/business phone thing. Every time I texted her in the past month, it seemed she was either on her way to a job, or just leaving a job.

"This guy Frederick from Malibu has been asking about you. He's, like, so fuckin' rich, girl." We were lying side by side in the sauna at our local Korean spa, relaxing after an anal threeway scene. The Korean spa is our secret little getaway. No one from porn knows about it, and on its worst day it's filled with Korean and Russian housewives who keep to themselves. This particular day was a weekday, and the sauna was empty except for us. Not that it would have made a difference if there were other people around. Laila is loud, crude, and gives a fuck about no one. Just that morning she had mortifyingly screamed across the line at a very crowded Starbucks, "Fuck Imodium, I drink coffee before anal!"

Normal.

It's inevitable. You can only show the inside of your asshole to the world for so long before your filter ceases to exist.

I wondered why she was bringing this guy up to me. She knew I wasn't into the escorting thing. This guy Frederick-from-Malibu was notorious for seeing girls in porn, a big-time CEO of a huge, very commercial, very family-friendly company.

"A few people hit me up about him. He sounds gross." It was true. He had been trying to get other girls to refer him to me since my early days in porn. "There's no way."

"He's super-nice and not gross at all. He'll pay you whatever you want."

"Tell him five thousand dollars for half an hour." Thinking this was a ridiculous deal no one would agree to, I laid a damp towel over my face and we proceeded to talk shit about the potential new girl in our agency. Spiegler was thinking of taking on a new Asian girl. As it stood, Laila and I were the only Asian girls on his roster. We wanted to keep it that way. He only represents twenty-five girls at a time, and so three of them being Asian would seriously dilute our market.

That night, Laila texted me. "He's in. When can you do it?"

Having no knowledge whatsoever regarding the world of hooking, yet feeling spontaneous, intrigued, and admittedly a little bored, I agreed to see Frederick-from-Malibu for half an hour the next evening, under one condition—that Laila come with me. I had no moral issue against escorting, just an irrational fear (. . . is it, though??) of being murdered. Two girls could take on one guy, right? Besides, the prospect of making my double penetration (one dick in the butt, one in the pussy) rate in a mere thirty minutes (without even putting anything in my ass) was too tempting. It was the length of a television show episode. Not even that long, if it were on HBO or Showtime. I persuaded myself to give it a try.

Laila drove. "Girl, it's so easy. You're gonna wonder why you didn't do this before."

"I don't know. What if he tries to pull something? I brought Mace. But it's fucking pink and I've never used it. Does Mace expire?"

"Shut up. We're gonna get there, have condom sex for ten minutes, shower, and leave. It's gonna be the easiest money you ever made."

Condom sex. Shit. I was so wrapped up in thinking of ways to hide my Mace within arm's reach during the actual fucking, I had totally forgotten to pack condoms. Rule number one as a working girl: Bring. Fucking. Condoms.

We weren't even there yet, and I already had one strike in the hooker game.

Luckily, Laila was more prepared than me. We got to the hotel, valeted the car, and took a fancy elevator up to the room. This is when things started getting real for me. Or maybe more like surreal. A million thoughts started racing through my head. Mainly, that if someone recognized us, they would for certain know what we were up to. And out us on the Internet. Or worse, call the cops. I turned my head down as much as I could without seeming too weird and silently cursed Laila for talking so damn loud. As we walked through the hallway I recognized the mirrors on the wall from various girls' self-taken cellphone photos on their Twitter profiles.

When Frederick opened the door, the first thing I noticed was that he was black. I had been hearing about this guy for years, and in my mind, he was white. Not like it really mattered. It's like that weird sensation when you pick up a drink thinking it's gonna be water, and as the liquid hits your tongue you realize it's Coca-Cola. Like everything you knew to be true a second ago is now questionable.

Frederick was wearing a white robe, I guessed with probably nothing underneath. He was much better-looking than I had expected. Handsome, even. Not old.

Not young, but not old.

He flashed a mouth full of expensive-looking, well-done veneers.

"I've been waiting to meet you. Come in."

When we entered the room, I saw he had a porno of mine playing on the TV. I was dressed up in what was porn's version of a schoolgirl outfit, and fucking my teacher for extra credit. Right away I noticed how horrible my skin looked on the huge screen.

I already regretted coming.

"I laid out some outfits for you girls in the bathroom," Frederick said.

Laila was clearly feeling more comfortable than me, making herself at home on the floor in front of the minibar. She got her drink, and we went into the bathroom. Just like he said, there were four schoolgirl uniforms laid out on the counter for us to choose from. They looked freshly dry cleaned, but definitely not new. Which girls had worn these outfits before me? Surely, I knew at least a few of them.

I chose a cropped collared shirt that showed off my stomach, and a red plaid skirt that came with a matching tie of the same pattern. I opted for the baggy Japanese-style leg warmer socks rather than the stockings. My shoes, I had brought. Laila picked a similar outfit in blue, only she went for the stockings. After dressing in silence, Laila put my hand in hers. We walked out together like this, hand in hand. I never asked her if she did this to comfort me, or as a part of the act. Either way, it was sweet.

The porno was still on the screen, but it wasn't my scene anymore. "Teacher, you wanted to see us? Is this about our recent tardiness?" Laila is a fucking pro.

"I hope you didn't call us in to punish us. We really are very good girls." I was shocked to hear my own voice chime in on this role play. The inner dialogue running in my head was far different. *Shit, I left my Mace in the bathroom. What kind of teacher wears a fucking robe? This is corny. Maybe it's not too late to go grab my Mace. I could say I have to pee.*

"Maybe Teacher can tell us how to work to our full potential." My mouth was making words that must have been ingrained into my brain from all the schoolgirl scenes I had shot over the years.

"You're good girls. Teacher thought you might like to earn some extra credit."

In this moment, I realized that people are actually into these tired, old, clichéd porno scenarios. Every time I shoot a student/teacher scene, I'm baffled at how the scripts never change. On the other hand, seeing how into the scene he was put me at ease. I probably didn't need my Mace.

I hoped my lack of enthusiasm wasn't too obvious.

We bent over against the TV screen and showed off our asses.

"Like this, Teacher?"

"Is this what you want? Does this make Teacher's cock hard?"

"Why don't you girls kiss each other? Put on a show for Teacher." Frederick sat on the sofa and stroked his dick while watching us. His cock was rock hard. I couldn't believe this cheesy half-assed act was working.

With my eye on Frederick, I kissed Laila as I put my hand on her pussy. I could tell immediately from the change in his breath that it drove him crazy.

And it dawned on me. Here we were, two girls he had been jerking off to for years. We were making this man's fantasy come true. In his eyes we could do no wrong. Everything we did was sexy. He had been waiting for this to happen for who knows how long. We were on a pedestal.

He was so obsessed with me that he was willing to pay for thirty lousy minutes with me.

I was starstruck on myself.

I was starting to enjoy this.

In true porno style, as if it were second nature to us, Laila and I dropped down to our knees in sync and crawled over to him on the sofa. I took his shaft in my mouth while she took the balls. I thought about how many times he had cum thinking about this moment.

Often, I think about the guy on the other side of the screen while I'm shooting. If I'm not particularly fond of my partner for the day, I know I can rely on the idea of the guy at home watching, jerking off to me to get me wet. Right now, right here, this was my favorite part of my job coming to life.

"Teacher, I want to be your favorite student."

By the time the condom was on and he put his dick in me, I was soaking wet. I screamed like I did in the movies for him. I shook my ass. Laila and I slapped each other around, just like we had done so many times before on camera. Only this time we had a live audience.

Like Laila had said, once we started fucking, it lasted about ten minutes. Like in the scene he was watching earlier, he came on our faces. We went to the bathroom, took turns showering, got our money, and left.

She was right. It was the easiest money I had ever made.

I saw Frederick again, on my own, the next day. We acted out a similar scenario, minus Laila. The sequel felt underwhelming. Maybe because I was alone . . . maybe because the novelty had worn off. Maybe because he wanted me to wear the same outfit as the day before, and it hadn't been washed. Or maybe it was the fact that he had asked me to fuck without a condom on, which just reminded me of how many girls in this business are fucking their clients raw. It made me sad. It turned me off. I never saw him again. He texts me from time to time, but I never reply. What's the point? The spark I felt on our initial rendezvous had gone. I had given the guy too much credit. Strike two.

Feeling confident about the gig, but not necessarily needing to experience it again, I told Laila hooking wasn't my thing. So the next time she mentioned a client, I smiled and told her, "Tell him ten grand."

I was joking. I never thought someone would pay that much for sex.

But Joe did.

The agreement was that I would meet him for dinner. If I felt uncomfortable in any way, I would walk away right there with a thousand dollars. If I went home with him, I'd get ten grand up front, cash. The holidays were just around the corner. It was an offer I couldn't turn down.

"I watch about five hours of porn a day," Joe confessed to me at dinner. His brutal honesty charmed me. Most people would consider this the kind of information you kept hidden on a first date. Then again, this wasn't a date. Like Frederick, he was kind of handsome. He was the kind of guy I'd like to watch a character-driven documentary on. Nerdy, socially awkward, and though I'm no psychologist, to me he seemed like he could be on the Asperger spectrum. After dinner I was more than thrilled to go back to his place. We stayed up all night and talked. Joe was smart, and I felt like I could listen to him talk forever. He was the kind of guy I could really *learn* from. I told him I had only hooked once (half true), and we were so enthralled in conversation, we didn't even get to fucking until five in the morning.

I think the *True Romance*–ness of it was what drew me in.

After the sex, we took a nap, went out to breakfast, and I drove home. I couldn't shake him off; I was fascinated by him, his brain, the whole scenario. I romanticized the situation, fantasized what it would be like if he were my Captain-Save-A-Ho.

The next week was Christmas, so my schedule was clear of shoots. Joe took me on a first-class trip to Hawaii. Everything was top-notch. The resort, our suite, our limos, everything. He worked the whole time we were there from his computer but had rented out a cabana for me by the pool for every day we were there. I lounged by the pool, went hiking, explored the resort, and shopped with his money while he worked all day. Then we'd meet up for dinner, fuck in the room after, and stay up late talking. It was perfect.

On the last night, we took a stroll along the beach after another fancy dinner. "How much longer do you want to do porn?" It was happening. The inevitable question. What it translates to is *I don't want to say it now but eventually I will ask you to quit your job for me.* Every guy I've dated has eventually brought this up; it's not a matter of if they will, it's a matter of when.

I imagined what my life would be like if I were with this guy. Could I really give up this life I was living? Sure, he was rich. I'd probably never have to work again. Ultimately, though, I knew what our destiny would be. I'd been down this road before. The first step would be for me to make faraway promises I knew at the bottom of my heart I couldn't keep. Then when the time came, I'd come to my senses and realize that I wasn't ready to give up my dream job. We'd argue, both make compromises, only to realize that our relationship would never work because ultimately I need to do what makes me happy, which is porn. We'd part ways and never speak again.

We didn't fuck that night. I hardly even spoke to him after he asked that question. He knew what my silence meant. The next day we flew back to Los Angeles. We said an awkward goodbye at the airport, and I knew I'd probably never speak to him again.

On the cab drive home, the first song to come on my iPod was "Ho," by Ludacris. What the fuck. Then I remembered a joke my friend Sebastian had told me a long time ago.

"You don't pay a hooker to come, you pay a hooker to leave."

I was the ultimate hooker failure. I didn't leave. At all. I did just the opposite. I came, over and over. I got emotionally involved and tried to make something out of nothing. Strike. Three.

Letter to Mom

August 12, 2008

Dear Mom,

California is great! The weather is beautiful, I mean it's August so that's obvious—but even when I got here five months ago, I was already laying out by the pool at the model house almost every day. There's five of us living here, in total—the agency, it's called Goldstar Modeling, has a house that girls from out of town can stay at.

The rest of the girls are all from random places like Ohio and Michigan. A couple of them make me feel like I need to keep a constant eye on my belongings, but for the most part, everyone is cool!

So far, I've found the stereotype of a typical porn-star . . . is kind of accurate. But also totally wrong. I mean there are definitely girls hooked on drugs, girls who have been abused by family members, girls who got in the business because their boyfriends, aka "suitcase pimps," wanted them to. But that's only about half of them; there are also girls with college degrees, girls who are feminists, and girls who come from completely normal backgrounds. My agent told me the former group won't last long; the latter is the kind that will be around in a few years. (This makes me feel confident.)

This one girl here, Devon, she's from Detroit. She's brand-new too. One day I was about to leave to the grocery store, which is like a ten-minute walk away. She asked me to pick up a sandwich for her (which was kind of annoying), so I was like, "Why don't you come with me?"

She was like, "I can't, 'cause I can't walk very far."

I was like, "It's not even ten minutes. Come on, don't be lazy—if anything it'll be a mini workout."

She was like, "Ever since I got shot, it hurts when I walk uphill."

(The walk on the way back is pretty much all on an incline.)

I asked her why she got shot. I thought . . . Detroit? Ghetto, right? Probably domestic abuse, or a drug-related thing.

She goes, "I got in a fight over a parking space, and the guy shot me in both of my knees."

Like holy fuck, Mom—I couldn't believe my ears! Who shoots someone—multiple times—over a parking spot????

So there's definitely that crowd.

My first week here was already pretty hectic. I mean the very day I arrived, my agent picked me up from the airport and drove me straight to a photographer to take my photos for the agency website. My agent is kind of weird. I mean I know he's legit cause Gina Lynn referred me to him, and he represents her, and she's one of the biggest stars around but . . . I think I'll just take everything he says with a grain of salt.

The next day, before my photos even went up, I went to meet with the owner of this company called Vouyer Media; and he signed me to an exclusive contract for my first few movies! It's a Gonzo company. See Mom, in porn, there are two kinds of productions: Gonzo porn, and Feature porn. In Gonzo, the movies are just straight-up sex—no dialogue, no setup, no scenario. The cameraman uses the camera to maneuver around the people having sex, getting really tight shots of the penetration and stuff.

Feature porn is totally different. It's considered "classier"—they are like real movies, but with sex scenes integrated into them. There are additional days of shooting only dialogue, and it's a really long and tedious process. The sex is usually way softer, too—and the camera generally stays on either a tripod or a jib, a safe distance away from the actual sex. It's marketed more toward couples and women.

Anyway, so my first five movies out were with Vouyer Media. They're already all out; Gonzo productions turn over pretty fast. It takes one day, about eight hours, to shoot a scene. The day starts out around 9 a.m. in the makeup chair. After that, we shoot "pretty girls," which are basically just photos of me by myself. I start out in the outfit appropriate for the day—doctor's outfit, schoolgirl uniform, office-wear, etc. . . . And then I strip down to my matching lingerie set, then to just me naked, and then they take close-up shots of my lady bits. Around 1 p.m., I put my lingerie and outfit back on, and we start shooting the tease, which is like a striptease, or "pre-sex" clip that gets edited down to four minutes total. That takes about an hour to shoot, until 2 p.m. when the male talent arrives. We shoot photos of 3–4 sex positions. By 3 p.m. we are usually ready to roll video on the sex, which lasts about thirty minutes. I'm usually showered and out the door by 5 p.m.

My second month of shooting, though, something kind of shitty happened. Are you sitting down? If not, sit down. This is gonna sound crazy to you I'm sure, but I promise you it's not a big deal. It's like catching a cold, really. I got chlamydia. It's curable! You just take a few pills and it goes away. But when they called me, I was totally devastated. I mean . . . It's an STD. Gross! Don't tell any of my friends, or your friends, okay? Don't even tell Dad. Just don't tell anyone please. We have this testing system out here, everyone in porn uses it. Every production company requires a test no older than thirty days (some require tests no older than fourteen days) to shoot a scene. It's pretty cool—at first I couldn't even look at the needle going into my arm, but now I hardly even notice when they poke it in. Anyways, I was at the beach with Jenna (she is staying at the model house too) when I got the call from them. The caller ID showed it was the testing facility, and Jenna immediately told me that was a bad sign, that they never call unless they have bad news.

"Hi, is this Asa?"

"Yeah, is everything okay?"

"I have some bad news, honey, it's about your test. You came up positive for chlamydia."

Mom, I swear, everything went dark after that. Like I know they always say that in books and movies and stuff, but it literally happened to me. I felt like I was about to pass out (I didn't), and Jenna had to call our agent for me. I think I was even deaf for a couple of minutes.

Anyways, Jenna drove me to the testing center, I took my meds on the spot, got retested a week later, and then I was ready to get back to shooting.

My first few scenes are kind of a blur. One of them was for a movie called "Make Me Creamy," and it's a cream-pie movie. Do you know what that is? It's when the guy cums inside the girl's vagina. I don't think I'm gonna do any more scenes like that. I mean I don't necessarily regret it, but . . . I just don't want random guys' sperm in me, you know?

So far, since those initial five movies I shot for Vouyer Media, I've done about fifty movies for different companies. That sounds like a lot, when I think about it. I think I like the Gonzo movies better—I think hardcore sex is what I'm really good at, you know? The acting stuff, I need some more practice with.

Oh, you wanna know something really weird? Black guys in porn don't take their shoes off during sex. Like if the scene starts off with them naked, they enter the frame fully unclothed, but with their shoes on. And if the scene starts with them clothed, they take off the shoes to remove their pants, and then THEY PUT THEIR SHOES BACK ON. And it's literally only the black guys. I'm gonna get down to the bottom of this before I leave the business.

Hmmm, what else have I learned . . . I learned that when I'm on my period, I can just cut off a little piece of a makeup sponge, stuff it deep in my vagina, and then I can still have clean, blood-free sex! I just have to make sure I take it out right after the scene—I accidentally left one in for two days once, and when I took it out, it smelled horrid.

Mom, I really feel like I've found my calling here. I know it's not what you want to hear—I know it sounds absolutely absurd. But the more I do this, the more I realize I'm exactly where I'm supposed to be. I hope you can be happy for me.

Write back!

I'll come home as soon as I can,

Love you,
Asa

Haiku

Home from Trader Joe's,

Was it there for that whole time?

Dried cum on my chin.

3
Penis Envy

Ruby and I sat on the floor of Studio E as we rehearsed our script. We were shooting a lesbian scene for BigTitsAtWork. com.

"What? You're not going to comment on my tits, Miss Akira?"

"Um, I think that would be inappropriate, boss."

"Well, if you're saying I'm distracting you from your work, and you want me to put these tits away, you're going to have to do it for me."

"I'm not sure that would be the right thing to do."

"Listen. If you want to keep your job, you'll do as I say. Now close the door and come be a good girl."

Scripts for these scenes never change much. Wardrobe is always a pencil skirt, stockings, and a collared shirt unbuttoned far too low for an actual office. There is always a boss, as well as an employee. The employee is generally at risk of losing their job. The sex, being part of a website centered around big tits in the office, involves a lot of breast play, and positions in which they are on full display. I always feel silly shooting for this site, since I don't have particularly large breasts; I always imagine the viewers at home wondering what I'm doing on this site. For some reason I imagine a British couple watching. The man would exclaim in the

Queen's English, "Look here, this girl is barely a C cup. What on earth is she doing here?"

"Who does she think she is?" his wife would answer, in an equally British accent. "Does she really think her breasts are big? That's preposterous!"

The couple would then toast with their wineglasses and have a good laugh at my expense.

As Ruby and I went over our lines over again, Brent came running in. He was the director of this fine website.

"They're shooting a gay scene next door in Studio D!" he burst.

In no way was his enthusiasm an overreaction. The gay and straight sides of porn rarely cross, and to us, on the straight side, the other side was a mystery land we knew nothing about. To be in the studio next to a gay scene being shot was like winning the freak show lottery.

We had all heard rumors of the other side.

"They don't get tested every month like us. They just use condoms."

"Seventy-five percent of them are HIV positive."

"I heard most of them are straight, they're just gay for pay. They all watch straight porn on their phones to get hard, and then shoot two minutes of sex at a time. That's how long they can keep their dicks hard."

I could hardly contain myself. Shooting up from my seat on the floor, I stood up, kicked off my heels, and ran to the door. There was no one standing outside their studio, not even taking a smoke break. I ran back to Brent. "How do you know? Where are they? Did you see them actually shooting?" I couldn't ask my questions fast enough.

"I went to pay Laura the studio fee, and they were there. Rocky's shooting his first bottom scene!"

What? Everything changed in one moment. Rocky, better known to me as Luke, was my ex-boyfriend. We were even briefly engaged for a month or two. I knew he was shooting gay scenes now, but never so physically close to me. The situation went from level *highly entertaining* to *awkward* in a flash.

Luke always denied being gay when we were together, but he liked to be fucked in the ass with a strapon. It's actually what drew me toward him in the first place. Physically, I suppose he looked like he could swing either way. Tall, muscular, not quite handsome, but passable as an overall good-looking dude. We worked together on a movie and exchanged numbers upon wrapping. I didn't know about his fetish at the time, nor was I really considering calling him, ever. I guess I was just being nice. Totally the opposite of my type, Luke was too *delicate*. Clean-shaven, manicured nails, perfect tan. The authenticity of his nose was questionable, and his teeth were undoubtedly too white to be natural. Originally a good country boy from North Carolina, soft-spoken and well mannered. He didn't *command* anything of me, which is something I usually needed in a man.

I've never been attracted to men who are anything but super-masculine. Things like body hair, mismatching clothes, and messy table manners are on the *Pros* side of the list. Men who act like men are hot—this new breed of "metrosexuals," with their Botoxed faces and tinted hair, did nothing for me.

Even the girls I find to be the hottest are the ones who look like men. With their short hair and taped-down boobs in wifebeaters, there's something so erotic about a girl acting like a guy. The whole overcompensated masculine energy thing is sexy.

I've often wondered if this just means I'm straight.

The truth is, I find women incredibly intimidating. When I see a sexy woman, right away I envision her looking at me in disgust as I approach her.

"Don't you think you're a little out of your league?" She'd laugh and go call a friend to make fun of me.

Women are beautiful, and I love pleasing them. Often, during a lesbian scene, I'll make a competition out of the sex. I like to see how good I can make her feel, how many times I can make her cum. I try to sync us in a way that we are riding the same sexual wave. The more resistant she is, the more fun my game becomes.

Fucking the shit out of a woman is enjoyable, but it's mashed potatoes—the delicious extra something on the side. The main dish has to be a man. I don't see myself ever dating a woman, or feeling a deep emotional connection to a woman I'm having sex with, either. Whenever I'm asked what my "type" is for females, I give different answers.

"Skinny with big boobs."

"The thicker the better."

"Teenaged Puerto Ricans with big asses."

I don't know why I feel this immense pressure to give a fake answer, when secretly my answer is, "I don't have a type. I like any girl that likes me."

After we exchanged numbers, Luke texted me incessantly. I only replied when I was bored—I gave him short answers, just enough to keep him interested. Nothing is more of a turnoff than when someone you're not into texts you. Of course, you could always just tell them you're uninterested, or ignore them altogether until they go away. Somewhere deep down, though, the attention is appreciated. At any given time, I always have a rotation of at least three guys, who I know I'll never give a chance to, but I keep them just interested enough so they'll stroke my ego from time to time. Call me insecure, but . . . Whatever works.

Months went by, and he was still texting me. My phone went off one day just as I was about to enter a tanning bed. I looked down. It was Luke. *Again.* I opened the message, thinking about what a pain in my ass he was, and not the good kind.

"Do u like using a strapon on a guy?"

The message caught me off guard. I delayed going into the tanning bed to reply.

"Yah. Y?"

"I saw a cover of u w a big black strapon. I like that too. But not on camera."

Whoa. This guy was finally starting to interest me. I would never have guessed he was the type. It all made sense now— that was why he was so *desperate.* He's a fucking sub.

"That's hot :)"

I had never worn a strapon in my personal life. For work, yes . . . but never just for fun. I was intrigued.

"Send me ur address. I'm coming over tonight to rape u. U better be ready. If u shit on my cock I'm leaving."

It was a date.

The last time I had fucked a guy with a strapon was for a scene in *Strap Attack 7.* Jeremy was submissive in his personal life, and he was eager for me to fuck him. It was something I had never done on camera, but I had done it numerous times at the dungeon—I assumed it would be easy. I was wrong.

"Open up to me please, Asa. I can't see the penetration."

"Move your hand, you're blocking his ass."

"Try to balance on your left leg so your hips open up; I can't see the dildo."

"Energy, Asa, I need more energy!"

By the end of the scene, my legs were on fire. At least five times, I needed to cut to take a break. I work out every day, eat healthy, and don't drink or party. Being the man in the scene was more work than I had realized. I was dripping sweat from constantly thrusting back and forth, and my back hurt from all the crazy positions I had to do in order for the camera to catch the action. Guys have to do all this while keeping their dicks hard? I had a newfound appreciation for male performers that day; as a girl, on our worst day, we can just throw some lube in, lie there, and get manhandled. The scene will still look good, as long as we can hold still in a few positions, and occasionally throw in a generic phrase like "Your cock is so hard in me," or "My pussy is so wet for you."

This shoot was good for me—it was both humbling and educational.

Personally, I don't really like to be fucked with a strapon. Dildos have never really done much for me; when I'm with a girl, I like for her to use what she already has. The hardness and rubberiness of a dildo make it feel unauthentic and painful. It's almost like the strapon puts too much distance between us. I like for us to feel close—fingers, hands, mouth, feet, knees, whatever. Sex with a girl, for me, is not about dominance or submission; rather, more about just feeling good.

On the other hand, when I'm the one *wearing* a strapon, something comes over me. I get on a high. It's something like being drunk with power—the things I say, the things I demand of my partner, are things I wouldn't dare dream of voicing in my normal state. With a strapon, I feel invincible. I feel like I could take over the world.

Once the strapon comes off, I feel embarrassed. If I felt that kind of power from simply putting a fake penis on, it's frightening to imagine the kind of corruption I'd really be capable of if I was someday in a real position of power. Why did I say those things? Who did I think I was?

That first night with Luke, I went on my usual power trip.

"You stupid faggot, you're so pathetic, aren't you? That's why you couldn't stop calling me. You had to beg for me to come fuck your ass just so you could see me."

It was a rush I hadn't felt since my domming days. The only difference was, the power trip didn't end when I removed the strapon. Instead, it continued on for over a year. I degraded and emasculated him on a daily basis. I wasn't happy in the relationship, but it was as if the meaner I was to him, the more he loved me; and the more he loved me, the more I needed him. Before I knew it, I was stuck. This man was so desperate for me, loved me so much, and would do anything for me. Never was I going to find someone like this again.

Of course, what we were feeling wasn't really love. It was our insecurities playing out in the most fucked-up, counterproductive way. He didn't love himself, and thought an asshole of a girlfriend like me is what he deserved. I, for the first time in my life, felt like I was in total control, and I couldn't let it go, no matter how much I didn't respect him, no matter that I didn't even like him.

That's my Google-based diagnosis.

Shortly after we started dating, I found out that Luke's fetish was no secret. People confronted me on almost every set and asked about our bedroom activities.

"Is it always dildos, or do you ever use vegetables?"

"Does he wear your underwear?"

"Do you ever make him suck it?"

The most common one was, of course, "Is he gay?"

"You're so close-minded," I would tell people. "Just cause he likes his *girlfriend* to fuck his ass with a strapon, it doesn't mean he wants an actual penis in him." People could be so dumb. In this day and age, you would think they could see past boxed, constrained labels. As little respect I had for Luke, I always defended him in this department. When it came to this issue, we were on the same team. It was more a matter of *principle* than anything. People needed to be educated.

Nothing turned Luke on more than when I called him a *faggot*. Maybe this was a clue I should've paid more attention to, but I always assumed it was the humiliation aspect that he liked. I never did ask him straight-up if he was gay, but I didn't feel the need to. He loved *me*. He wanted *me* to fuck him. What could possibly be gay about that? A part of me also didn't want to know if he was, in fact, batting for the other team. I had a boyfriend who was basically my slave. In the time we were together, I never paid for anything, filled my car with gas, or cooked for myself once. This was heaven. So what if other people judged our relationship? It was a small price to pay.

I got used to ignoring the gay rumors pretty fast, but Dan was the worst. It was always "your gay boyfriend this," "your gay boyfriend that," all day long whenever I shot for him. To this day, his set is the only one I've ever walked off without completing my job.

We shot all the nonsex stuff first, which took about six hours. I started the day off laughing the jokes off, but as the day got later and my sugar levels dropped (it was an anal day—restricted food), my patience wore out. Right as I went to rinse my butt out with an enema for the actual sex scene, Dan called out, "Don't worry, Johnny, her asshole isn't gonna turn you gay, too."

It was a stupid joke that didn't even make sense. But I had had enough.

"Fuck this shit." I kicked my porno stilettos straight into my suitcase and started to undress out of my outfit. I don't think I've ever gotten dressed so fast. It was unfortunate, too—my outfit for the day was a bathrobe, which is like hitting the porno lottery. Usually we're in elaborate lingerie or dresses—an outfit as simple or comfortable as a robe comes but a few times in a career.

"Asa, come on, we're all friends here. I'm just kidding." Dan started to get nervous. I could see in his face, he was calculating how much money this shoot had already cost—if he didn't get the sex, it would all be worth nothing.

"I'm not starving myself all day so I can take a cock up my ass for you! You're an idiot. You just wasted everyone's fucking time!"

I stormed off set. It takes a lot to get me that mad, but Dan had done it. I was tired of people trying to tell me the sexual orientation of *my* boyfriend. No one was going to tell me my boyfriend was gay anymore. In an industry where we were so often shunned from society because of our sexuality, you would think people would be more open-minded and understanding. It made me sick.

So imagine my surprise when Luke signed a yearlong contract with Men.com. We had already been broken up for well over a year, and hardly ran into each other. Things had ended on a sour note, when one day he confessed to me everything he had ever told me was a lie. The reason he liked strapons in his ass was *not* because his stepfather had raped him. His last name was not pronounced "Brah-may," but rather "Broom," as in "broomstick," just like it was spelled phonetically, "Broome." And that time I rushed home from my webmaster's birthday party because Luke's mother had unexpectedly died? Not true, she was well and alive.

I had been the last girl he dated before venturing into the other side of porn.

The press release came out while I was on set, starring in a weeklong feature with a company that had hired Luke many, many times over the years. No one wanted to talk to me about it, let alone look me in the eye for the remainder of the shoot. It was too awkward. I immediately texted everyone I knew in the business, "Do me a favor and spare me the 'I told you so.'"

As Ruby and I shot take fourteen of our office dialogue, we heard banging from the other side of the wall. For a studio, the walls were fucking thin. I heard everyone chuckle. I looked up, and they nervously covered their mouths and gazed in random directions.

Brent didn't crack a joke. "All right, let's do another take for sound. Rolling, and action."

4

Nutcracker Suite

Mistress. After almost a year of dominating men at the Nutcracker Suite, I still wasn't able to get used to the title. Baby Sean, Ronnie the Tooth Guy, Eli the Trustfund Kid . . . They all called me that. Yet I never felt quite comfortable saying it myself.

I was one of five dominatrices on duty at any given time. The Nutcracker Suite was one of the few reputable dungeons in the city, managed by Clint, who rode to work on a Harley. Clint didn't look like your typical submissive dungeon manager; with his leather motorcycle jacket, long hair, missing tooth, Brillo-looking beard, and all-black-everything uniform, he looked more like an ugly member of the Hells Angels. Despite all this, Clint was into some of the most hardcore shit I've ever seen in my whole life. I stuck a metal rod inside his urethra and electrocuted him once. He asked me to, one night when it was slow.

"See this dial here? To the right is stronger. Put it in first and start low." The rod was about five inches long, and thin, like a barbecue skewer. Although, can you really consider anything thin when it's going into your dick hole? "Here, put it in."

I did as he said.

As soon as I put the tip in, his hole just sucked in three quarters of the rod. I couldn't believe how easily it went in.

(Later, I would learn this isn't always the case. Urethras are like assholes. The more times it's been penetrated, the less time it takes to open up.)

Clint was already in ecstasy.

I slid the metal in and out without turning the electricity on to see what his reaction would be. He smiled. His face looked like how I feel when a dick penetrates me.

Steadily as I could, I turned the dial on, and slowly nudged it to the right. The electricity started buzzing right away. It got louder and louder with every millimeter I turned. Curious, I put my hand around his cock and felt the electricity in my fingers, through my hand, and up my wrist. It didn't hurt. Unlike the sharp sensation I expected it to be, it felt dull, like my hand had fallen asleep. Of course, I wasn't holding the metal directly. I had a penis buffering the static.

The device turned me on a little bit. It scared me, but it would be a lie to say I wasn't getting wet. Feeling the excitement, yet aware that I was electrocuting a man, I kept my hand on his dick and stayed nervous, still as a statue. Clint was twitching, but not in an overboard kind of way. I turned the dial again to the right.

He started yelling. "Fuck! FUCKKK!!" I was just about to rush to switch the machine off when he told me to go higher.

I held my breath and turned the dial again.

He kept yelling.

I couldn't breathe, or take my eyes off his face, which was morphing into something like Edvard Munch's most famous painting.

As subtly as I could, I grinded my pussy into the medical bed we were sitting on. I hoped Clint didn't notice.

Probably because I was holding my breath, I started to feel a little dizzy. As I tried to focus on my breath and calm myself down, Clint pulled the rod out himself, squeezed my hand over his cock, and jerked it till cum came pouring out on both of our hands.

I don't know how I left that room, but the next thing I remember is rubbing my pussy in the bathroom. I used the hand with Clint's cum on it.

It was the only time I touched a penis at the dungeon, and I felt dirty and disgusting. I saw something I was appalled by, yet somehow it was completely fascinating. I made myself climax as quietly as I could.

I turned on the sink and watched the cum on my hand turn into rubber when it hit the water. Something about cum, once it's cooled off, is just nauseating. Like my orange juice, it was something I only enjoyed freshly squeezed.

I flushed the toilet so no one would suspect anything. Clint was our "gross manager," and I didn't want him to think he turned me on.

He was hardcore like *that*.

At twenty years old, I was the youngest one at the dungeon, but not by much. No one was over thirty. The head bitch in charge was Mistress Rox. She had been there for eight years, and was known in the city as one of the meanest, baddest, yet most sensual masters. I've seen her shit on a guy. Like, right on his face. There's no way he didn't get pinkeye from that. You can't erase things like that from your memory, no matter how much you want to. It's like herpes in your brain. It's forever.

Rox is tall, even before she puts on her six-inch heeled boots every night. She had long black hair paired with a cold Eastern

Europe–esque face, and when she was sober, she could dominate like no one I had ever seen. The creativity, commands,
and insults that would come out of this woman's mouth were
unfathomable to my comparatively amateur mind. Throughout the last year I had seen her relapse into her heroin addic-
tion multiple times, and there was always a big drama to get
clean again. There were nights she would sit at Clint's desk
crying, all doped up, refusing to see a single client. "Tell him
to go fuck himself . . . I quit . . . I quit . . . I hate that pathetic
piece of shit . . . I want my sweetie . . . Clint, tell my sweetie
to come get me . . ."

Her refusal of service was ultimately for the best. Subs are
clients for life, if you want them to be. You can't let them see
you in any type of position but strong, or they'll find someone else to worship. Rox always bounced back up. She never
quit for long.

None of the other girls had been working longer than two
years. From what I've seen, it's not a job many can stick to
much longer than that. In the beginning, it's liberating. It's
the boyfriend you always wanted to beat the shit out of, the
boss you only thought you could be in your wildest dreams,
the carnival in town with the biggest collection of freak shows
you never knew existed. A whole new world to explore.

Clint had picked me up on the street—almost literally—
one night when I was walking back home with Eddie, my
then-husband, from a concert. I had a moderate-to-medium
OxyContin habit around that time, and there came a point at
the concert where I just didn't want to stand anymore. I had
convinced Eddie to leave early. Oxy is a versatile little pill, in
the sense that depending on how much you take, it can be

like five different drugs. You're in complete control of how high you are. Take a little, and you're a perfectly functioning human being. No one can tell you're on anything. Take a lot, and you're all "I think my eyes are open. Are my eyes open?"

That night I had only taken a little. When I was on this level of high, it was a common occurrence for me to be walking, talking, excuse myself to go throw up on the side of the street, wipe my mouth off, and then come back to the conversation like nothing had happened.

"You okay, Peanut?" Eddie yelled from the hot dog stand as I finished barfing on the side of a building. I could never understand how Eddie could eat on Oxy.

"Yah. One second." I was spitting out what was left in my mouth when Clint approached me.

"Excuse me, miss?" *Fuck. Tell me I didn't just puke on this man's wall.* "I'm sorry to bother you; can I ask you a question?"

"Sure." *Really? Now?*

"Would you be interested in working in the adult entertainment industry?" This guy was bold.

"Sure. Let me get my husband."

Dungeons always smell the same way. A base of rubbing alcohol, with high notes of metal and semen. I'm not the kind of person to walk into a room and claim, "Ooohhh, the *energy* in here is so *weird*," but let me tell you—the energy in a dungeon is fucking weird. It's almost like the air is a little thicker. Looking back, I can't believe we followed Clint upstairs, much less agreed to start training the next day. But I had always wanted to work in porn, or a stripclub, or do *something* in the adult world. Eddie, my friends, everyone around me knew that.

Day one, I was already in heaven. My first client was a pro baseball player.

"I want to role-play like we're on the subway. I'll like stare and stare at you, and you're like just totally creeped out by me."

My second client gave me an hourlong foot massage. Another guy wanted me to piss on him. Five clients in total booked me that night. I left feeling like I had found my calling.

I should mention now that I'm not sexually dominant in my personal life. Ironically, none of the girls working at Nutcracker were. Not even Rox. We were all submissive in nature, to one degree or another. At that point in my life, I didn't recognize myself as submissive or dominant. I just knew I liked to please.

Eventually, I met Ronnie, who had seen every dominatrix in the city. Every single one. He never saw the same one twice. It was bound to be my time sooner or later. Before I introduced myself, the girls let me in on what he was about.

Ronnie has a dentist fetish. And elephantiasis on one of his balls. Maybe it's not fair for me to label it as elephantiasis. But one of his balls is fucking huge.

Anyway, what Ronnie does is he brings in his own dentist kit to the session. He always books an hour and a half, never more, never less. He will try to persuade you to shoot his mouth up with Novocain, but from what I hear, he's only succeeded in getting two girls to go through with this.

When I walked into the medical room, Ronnie had already set himself up in the chair. The rumor is that he bought this chair himself and had donated it to the dungeon. I have yet to meet another client with a fetish involving a dentist chair, so this makes sense.

Ronnie had a bib around his neck, and his dentist kit was laid out on the counter for me.

"How are we feeling today, Ronnie?" I started.

"Hi, Doctor, I feel like there's a loose tooth. I think I need it looked at."

I slowly put on my latex gloves as I listened, even adding the snap at the bottom like I had seen in pornos.

"Open your mouth wide, say 'ahhh.'" I dug around his mouth and felt the latex squeak against his teeth. "Which tooth is the one we're concerned about, Ronnie?"

"The third molar from the back, on this side." He motioned his hand up to the left side of his face, the side I was on.

"I see." I wiggled the tooth in question. "This doesn't look good, Ronnie."

"Do you think you'll have to pull it out?" The sudden excitement in his voice was impossible to miss.

"I'm afraid so, Ronnie."

After that, I didn't know where to go. I mean I wasn't going to pull this man's tooth out. So I just repeated "It doesn't look good" over and over, and kept wiggling.

I did this for the entire session.

After he left, I was embarrassed at how my mind had failed me when I tried to think of more dentist things to say. To everyone's surprise, he came in for me again the next night. He had never booked anyone more than once. I don't know what I did right. I repeated the same exact session for the second night in a row.

Around that time, I also met Eli. Eli was a trust fund kid. He technically owned a dance company, but fundamentally, he didn't work. Almost every night, he would come in and book double, triple, sometimes quadruple sessions, back to back. To be honest, I don't really even think Eli is a sub. He liked his nipples pinched hard; as far as I knew, that was about the freakiest thing about him, sexually.

The thing about Eli that made him so special was that he smoked crack.

Growing up in New York City, I discovered drugs at a young age. I dropped Ecstasy for the first time at thirteen. By fourteen, I had tried every drug there was available to me, except crack and heroin. Acid, mushrooms, pharmaceuticals, angel dust, salvia, coke, speed . . . But Special K was my favorite. My best friend Dee and I would regularly buy a liq each day after school, cook it up at night, and snort the powder in the morning before leaving the house to make the subway ride to school enjoyable. That's how much I loved it. Somehow I never got physically addicted to anything, and I was fully sober (including alcohol!) by the time I was twenty-two. Starting drugs at such a young age, I think, was a blessing in my case. By the time I was an adult, I was over the whole partying scene, and ready to join reality.

Crack was something my circle had always looked down upon. We smoked weed every day and did harder drugs on a weekly basis, but crack and heroin were out of the question. Those drugs were for losers. We were above it.

I had never actually met a crackhead in real life. Nor did I have any desire to. In my mind, *crackhead* was somewhat synonymous to *homeless*.

When the girls told me about Eli, I couldn't believe what I was hearing. I didn't understand how Clint could let some disgusting lowlife, a *crackhead*, come under our roof. To think he let him smoke crack during the sessions—I just didn't get it.

Until I met him.

My first session with Eli I did as a favor to Clint. I walked into the torture room half expecting to meet a guy wearing a blanket and pushing a shopping cart. How could Clint let this guy book me? I went to a Manhattan *private school*, for crying out loud.

Eli took me by surprise. He was nothing how I had imagined—he was in sweats, but they were from Zegna. He wore a black carbon fiber Hublot watch I had never even seen before, that I knew cost at *least* $250,000. Definitely not handsome, but he didn't have the face of someone who was broke. Or broken.

This guy smokes crack?

The first few sessions I did with Eli, I just pinched his nipples and listened to him ramble for however long he had booked me. His stories bored me half to death. I dreaded his sessions.

His ideas were grandiose and unrealistic, and I never knew which of the things that he said were true, and which were lies or exaggerations. He offered me a hit at the beginning of every session and, most of the time, again halfway through. I always turned him down. I had no interest in smoking something that would make me act like *that*. Besides, I had my Oxy, and that was enough for me.

Then one night, I caved. I could sit here and endlessly list excuses. I was bored. My Oxy was wearing off. I got curious. He pressured me.

The truth is that I just did it, without any thought. He made his obligatory offer at the beginning of a session, and where I usually answered *No*, I blankly nodded *Yes*.

Describing the first time I smoked crack feels like describing the moment I discovered true happiness.

I smoked through a glass pipe and felt the thick smoke enter my chest. It's not like weed or tobacco smoke. More chemical-ish, the vapor is almost cold as it fills you. The moment you inhale it, you feel your reality shift instantaneously. As you hold the smoke in, you get higher and higher—it's as if you can literally feel the crack spreading to the rest of your body, starting at your lungs. One cell at a time, your body becomes a whole other being—a happier, lighter, more energized being. It's like waking up from a coma and your life is a whimsical musical number in a Disney movie.

"This is amazing," I heard myself telling Eli. "I can't stop smiling."

Eli was smiling back at me. "I told you."

In that moment, I loved him. I loved crack.

Just as those thoughts formed in my mind, I felt a little less high. Or was I imagining it? No, it was definitely happening. I was coming down. Every two seconds that passed, I felt my high slip away from me a little bit more. I held my breath in a panic, as if that would keep the crack from escaping my body. No. No. This wasn't fucking happening. It felt so good such a short amount of time ago. I looked to Eli. He knew what was happening. I needed another hit.

I saw why crack was considered the most dangerously addictive drug. The high is too good. Losing it is too painful.

Eli came in for sessions for the next two nights, and we got high together. It was miserable. I didn't sleep when I went home, my mouth was full of canker sores from nervously chewing my lips, and I never felt like I did that first time, no matter how many hits I took.

At the end of the third night of my crack binge, I lost it. I didn't act out in any way—in fact, I did just the opposite. It was hard to speak or move. I could walk from one end of the room to the other, but walking felt uncomfortable. Sitting down felt uncomfortable. Everything felt disgusting.

I managed to text Eddie, who was my *ex*-husband by that time. "*911. Come get me. At Nutcracker. Please.*"

Eddie picked me up in a cab. We weren't getting along at the time; we had separated only a few months ago after what seemed like an eternity of sucking the life and light out of each other's souls. The days of him calling me Peanut were long gone, and we rode in silence. I didn't tell him what was going on. It was dawn already; the sun was coming up. Something about that hour when night turns to day makes everything so much worse when you're on drugs. He took me back to the condo we had lived in together, and all I wanted to do was close all the curtains and crawl into bed, under the covers, with a Xanax. Alone.

I ran upstairs to the bedroom. The blackout curtains were closed. Thank God. I looked in Eddie's underwear drawer and found a bottle of Xanax. Double thank God. I dived into the bed.

Something felt wrong. *What the fuck? Are the sheets wet?* I couldn't decide if I was imagining things. The sheets felt damp and cold. *Had I fucking pissed myself?*

I got up, turned on the light, and pulled my panties down. Bone dry. I put my hand on the sheet. It definitely felt wet.

I yelled downstairs. "Am I crazy, or are the fucking sheets wet??" Communicating took so much effort. There was no room for me to use my manners.

"I washed them earlier; when I took them out of the dryer they were still wet—I thought I'd let them dry on the bed."

Are you. Fucking. Kidding me. Right there I started to cry. Shit like this only happens when you're high as fuck.

Men are such morons, the Xanax hasn't kicked in yet, and all I want is a bed. "Get the fuck up here!" I screamed down to Eddie, who was already heading upstairs to me.

"What the fuck is your problem? Yo, what are you even doing here?" Eddie's New York Puerto Rican accent always came out more when he was mad.

"I fucking smoked crack, you asshole! All I want is a fucking bed and some peace and quiet, and you had to be so fucking stupid and put WET SHEETS on the bed! Now the mattress is wet and there's nowhere to fucking sleep! And I'm fucking coming down from crack!" I could hear myself yelling like a legitimate crazy person, but I didn't care. "Just GET THE FUCK OUT!"

Eddie was laughing at me, which enraged me even more. He turned around and left the room. I slammed the door behind him. I was so fucking mad. And all I wanted to do was curl up under the motherfucking covers and have a moment of peace. I was so damn *uncomfortable*.

I walked to Eddie's closet and started throwing all of his clothes on the floor. I made sure to make enough noise for him to know I was fucking shit up. I stomped unnecessarily

and rattled the drawers. I left nothing hanging. I turned off
the lights, lay down on the mountain of sweaters, shirts, and
pants, and put his robe over me. I buried my face into Eddie's
clothing and screamed into the pile.

The Xanax finally kicked in.

It would be another year before I got sober, but that was
the last time I smoked crack. Eddie went to jail shortly after,
when his bookkeeping business got busted. He called me the
other day, collect. I asked him if he remembered the time I
smoked crack and acted like a mental patient.

"Yo, you were always the best, Peanut," he laughed. "I'm
proud of you."

5
Liar Liar

Halfway through my second year in porn, when my career was really starting to take off, I started to get bad acne. It was the cystic kind that covers the entire face, the kind of acne where you see someone, and it's the first thing you notice about them. Eventually I got to the point where it put me in such a deep depression that I didn't leave the house unless it was for work. I blamed porn. Every day, a different makeup chair. Thick layers of product caked onto my skin, only to sweat half of it off during the sex scene. I'd have to get back into the makeup chair, and get more product caked back on over my sweat to shoot the rest of the scene.

It was crippling. It hurt my feelings. I felt betrayed. How could you, Porn? I love you. I do everything you ask for. When you wanted to see me put my fist inside my vagina, I did that. You want to inspect my asshole using a speculum? Sure, why not. Double anal? You got it!

I gave you everything. In return, you gave me a disfiguring rash on my face.

I kept hoping time would make it would go away, but it didn't. Thousands of dollars were spent on spa treatments, expensive creams and lotions, homeopathic remedies. Reluctantly, I even tried to slow down on shooting in hopes it would get better. Acne is especially bad for porn; between rubbing spit-covered cocks all around my mouth, making out, getting my face smooshed into furniture, and sweating like a pig under the hot lights, the makeup never manages to stay on. I'd start off the scene looking like a pornstar, and end it looking like a monster. No one was saying it out loud, but I knew I was losing work because of my skin.

During this miserable time in my life, I got booked for a softcore movie for a big cable network series. Shooting a softcore movie is completely different from shooting a hardcore one, which is what I usually have the pleasure of doing. Once or twice a year, I'll agree to these "Skinemax" type projects, but every time I get to the set, I remember: "Oh yeah. I hate this shit."

The first thing about these softcore productions that makes me want to shoot myself in the face is that the cast consists mostly of mainstream actors, meaning, they don't do actual porn. They are aspiring "real" actors who happen to be comfortable showing nudity. This is just a pit stop on their way to achieving their dreams.

Which, by itself, is fine.

Except that now, it leaves me to be the target of their objection. I'm the smelly kid in the class. I become the one who no one wants to stand near, in fear that they will catch my New and Improved Airborne Super-AIDS.

Second, and perhaps this is the main thing, there is no real sex.

Like, not even with a condom.

We are shooting simulated sex—actual penetration never happens. We have to wear these paperlike G-strings (guys included) so that our genitals never even touch. The whole reason I got into porn in the first place was for the sex. *What is this bullshit? It's certainly not what I signed up for* is usually my secret mood by the end of the day on one of these jobs. Every moan and scream is dishonest, and something about knowing I have to *pretend* I'm getting fucked, when I'm really not, makes me say stupid and outlandish things like "*My little pink pussy feels like a flower giving birth to your big beautiful rocket!*" or "*Fill my gushing river of a pussy up, you sexy bastard.*"

I've never been good at lying.

So my skin was making me hate life, and I was on a set where everyone thought I was disgusting, when Roger, the director of this stupid softcore production, asked me to stay after everyone had left. *Great.*

This is another thing I hate about softcore sets. I'm automatically assigned the role of "resident slutface," and I have to explain (usually to the director or the producer) that I'm just there to do my job—which, on this particular set, as I'm all too aware of, is *not* to have sex. This hardly ever happens on a hardcore set; as the legendary Nina Hartley so eloquently puts it, "You don't fuck to get the job. Fucking *is* the job."

I mentally rehearsed my usual "I have a boyfriend, we don't sleep with anyone else outside of sex scenes" speech and entered the room Roger had set up to be his office.

"So you wanted to see me?" Roger was standing at the desk pretending to go through some paperwork. Typical.

"Can you shut the door? I want to talk to you in private."

I shut the door and walked closer to Roger, but not close enough where he could easily touch me. I wondered if there would ever come a time in my life where I wouldn't measure distance by the amount of time it would take for a person to physically come on to me.

"What's going on with your face?" Roger was looking at me dead in the eye.

I was surprised. "Wait, what?"

"Your face is practically unshootable. I don't even know if we can use any of your close-ups. It's not good. I know you're not on drugs. What's going on?"

I wanted to cry. "Is this what you called me in for?"

"Honey, you need to do something about that. This is your career we're talking about here. I can't hire you again until it's taken care of."

I wanted to punch him. One thing I despise above anything else is when people call me by pet names. It's condescending and gross. Did this guy realize how much of an asshole he was coming off as? I swallowed my pride and decided to get out of there before I really did start crying.

"Thanks. But I'm getting it taken care of. I gotta go, Yoga starts in thirty minutes."

After that day, I made the decision to go on Accutane. I had heard countless horrible things about the drug, but it was my last resort. Fucking Roger said I was unshootable. Dick.

Accutane is definitely a drug to be taken seriously. The little pills come individually wrapped, and on every single pill there's an image of a pregnant woman, with an X over her. I signed a contract promising I wouldn't get pregnant, and if I did, I would abort it. After googling "Accutane baby" and seeing horrifying things, I saw for myself why all this precaution was absolutely imperative.

Imagine the first woman to have a baby while on the drug. Like some poor lady with acne gets pregnant, she's all excited about starting a new life with her baby. Her face is probably finally starting to clear up, but BAM, when the baby is born, he has a head shaped like a fucking cone and eyes on the sides of his head like a damn horse. It's moments like this when I remind myself to be grateful that I have ten fingers, ten toes, and an (although bigger-than-average) normally shaped head.

My skin problem was fixed. Unfortunately, my hair was another story. Although, comparatively, my hair situation wasn't that bad, there's still no quick fix for porn-damaged hair. Once it's fried, it's fried, and you just have to wait for it to grow out.

Blow-dried, straightened, curled, teased. Every day. I don't know who suffers more—me, with my limp, breaking, dying hair, or Toni, my now husband, who has to look at my old Facebook photos *yet again* as I reminisce, "My hair was so *shiny*. Do u see? How *shiny*?"

When I remember to, I just suck it up and tell myself that split ends are a small price to pay to make a living having multiple anal orgasms.

I've had the same hairdresser for the entire time I've been in California. I'm an easy sell, so naturally, Rose loves me. Don't even bother asking me to count how many "New! Revolutionary! All the rage in Brazil!" useless treatments I've paid her for.

When I first met Rose, I had just moved to L.A. to really start making the porn thing happen.

"So what do you do, babe? You've been coming here for months and you never told me." Hairdressers always ask too

many questions. And she called me "babe." Ew. If I could find
a mute person to cut my hair, I'd be all over it. Unfortunately,
for now Rose was the only one who didn't cut too much off
when I asked for a trim. So I'd have to stick with her.

"I don't really work. I have a boyfriend that supports me."
Lie. I didn't even have a boyfriend then. But I didn't want to
tell her the truth. *What if she is a religious nut? Or a women's
rights activist? If she has something against porn, she might
fuck up my hair on purpose.* It was too much to risk. "I guess
I got lucky."

"Oh, that's nice. What does he do?"

"Oh, you know . . . He owns businesses and stuff." Nice.
Vague but doesn't make him sound like a loser.

"That's cool. What type of businesses?" Rose is relentless.

"I can't really talk about it. It's illegal." Did I really just say
that?

"Okay. So where are you from?"

"New York City." Finally, something I could talk about
without lying.

"So you came out here to be with your boyfriend?"

"I guess, something like that, yah." Er.

"Do you want to marry him?"

"I think so."

"Is he Asian?"

"No. Italian." Who am I?

Over the next three years, I continued to lie to Rose. She
asked so many damn questions, I started to get used to it.
I created a whole other persona, an entire alternate life in
which I was the fabulous girlfriend of a drug dealer. We lived
in Beverly Hills and had two dogs together. Somewhere along

the way, I started to lie way more than was necessary. I was offering information on nonexistent family members, vacations that had never happened, and how I had finally found my calling and was writing a novel. We even talked about porn once. I told her my boyfriend was too jealous to let me do anything like that.

I should have known better. I always get caught lying, which is why I try to do it as little as possible. The last big lie I had told was to my parents in 2007, that I was attending a college in Florida. What I was really doing there was working for a radio show as the "show whore" and dabbling in girl-on-girl porn. They found out.

One day, I went to shoot for a company that I had never worked for before. Late as usual, I rushed in. The makeup artist was already set up and waiting, so I apologized and sat straight into her chair.

In porn, the makeup artist usually does both face and hair. The hairstyles aren't all that elaborate, so it's not really a problem. Occasionally, the makeup artist will bring in an assistant to do the hair, and they'll split the rate paid by the company.

That was the case on this shoot. The makeup artist, whom I had never met, had brought someone. The assistant, who was set up on the other side of the room, looked familiar to me. I just assumed she had assisted someone else before.

She kept looking my way as I got my makeup done. After almost an hour of this, I deliberately didn't look in her direction, to avoid the awkwardness. She was making me self-conscious. It's like she wasn't even trying to be subtle about it. *What does this bitch want?*

When my makeup was done and it was time to get my hair done, I was sent into the assistant's chair.

"How've you been, babe." Holy shit. *Babe*. It was Rose.

". . . Oh my God, hey!" I stood up to give her a hug, mostly because I didn't know what else to do.

Maybe it was because I wasn't expecting to see her in this environment, but I swear I didn't recognize her. No wonder she looked familiar. She had been cutting my hair for the past three fucking years.

We didn't talk about it, but we both knew. It was too awkward for me to bring up. I wouldn't have known where to even begin.

I think she wanted to avoid embarrassing me. There were other people in the room. I'll always feel thankful to her for that.

I still see Rose. She's still the only one I trust to not cut off too much when I ask for a trim. She never asks me questions anymore. In fact, we hardly even speak except for when she asks me what I need for my hair. I suppose if I really wanted to, it wouldn't be so hard to tell her the truth now. "*I'm not writing a novel, I don't have an Italian drug dealer boyfriend, I live in the Valley and I've been in porn the whole time you've known me. But you knew that. I'm sorry, I never know what to tell people at first. I guess you know my secret now!*" We could probably have a laugh about it. She might even give me a discount due to our newfound camaraderie.

But why on earth would I do a thing like that?

I have finally gotten my mute hairdresser.

Haiku

Q-tip in my ear,

If my pussy were to break;

You would be enough.

6
Crime and Punishment

I was twelve years old when I discovered I didn't have to pay for things in order to own them. Attending the United Nations International School (UNIS) at the time, I was surrounded by the Manhattan elite. Spoiled trust fund babies, and children of diplomats who arrived to school in black limousines with special license plates. That's not to say personally I grew up particularly rich. My grandfather, before suffering a stroke and being confined to a wheelchair for the remainder of his life, served as a diplomat for forty-five years. UNIS granted me a scholarship, upon returning to New York City from six years spent in Tokyo.

"Come with me and Jenna after school," Georgia whispered in biology class. "We've been stealing Hello Kitty stuff from FAO Schwarz."

The idea of shoplifting, by itself, didn't really interest me. Georgia and Jenna were the most popular girls in the seventh grade, though, and I was still just the *new kid*. We were already halfway through the school year, but these kids had all known each other since preschool. It wasn't easy fitting in. I jumped at the chance.

"Okay. I gotta call my mom." I called from the pay phone in the cafeteria during lunch.

"Ask her if you can sleep over," Georgia mouthed to me.

When we got to FAO, we walked straight upstairs to the Hello Kitty section. Georgia and Jenna picked up any item they saw that sparked their interest, and didn't stop until they couldn't carry any more. I grabbed a few pens.

"C'mon, let's go to the escalator," Jenna said, and walked ahead of us.

"The elevator is the one spot there's no camera," Georgia explained out of the side of her mouth.

We went to the escalator and stuffed our findings into our schoolbags, then casually walked out of the store.

It was that easy. It was *too* easy.

Over the next six years, I would go shoplifting on a regular basis. Georgia and Jenna accepted me as the final piece to their trio, and we would go on sprees almost every day after school. We outgrew FAO Schwarz within a few weeks after that first day, and moved on to hit the stores in SoHo. Everywhere from the GAP to Ralph Lauren, there was no store too small or too big for us to take on. At the beginning of each session, we'd stop in a few high-end stores and ask for paper bags, claiming our school bag had broken, or we needed them for a project for social studies class. This way, when we entered the stores we were going to steal from, we looked like legitimate customers enjoying a day of shopping with Daddy's money. At twelve years old, I owned a $2,500 cashmere sweater from Ralph Lauren, which I washed in the washing machine at the local Laundromat.

We made games out of our trips. Some days were designated to finding gifts for each other. Instead of stealing for ourselves, we would only take things for the other two. At the end of the day, we would sit on the living room floor of

Jenna's townhouse in Gramercy Park and take turns presenting our gifts to each other, like Christmas morning. Jenna's dad owned a printing company, and her parents were never around; they owned a house in California and vacationed to Europe often. She and her sister basically were underage roommates living alone in one of the most coveted pieces of property in Manhattan.

It was only a matter of time before we found other opportunities to incorporate our newfound deviance. On weekends, we'd head to pet stores to buy crickets and bring them to restaurants. Never hitting the same place twice, at the end of our meal we'd bury a cricket in a plate of food.

"Excuse me. I can't be sure, but I think there's a bug in my food. I really don't want to make a scene, but could you take a look at this? Actually, could you call your manager over?" Taking turns acting as the victim, once the manager came we'd claim our father was a lawyer, and have our meals comped immediately. With our freshly stolen expensive clothes and high-end shopping bags, no one ever doubted us.

One night, after a long day of hustling, Jenna and I went out to dinner at a busy restaurant in the West Village. It was the kind of restaurant that doubles as a bar, and we had to speak directly into each other's ears just to be able to hear one another. We hadn't planned on anything, not even a dine-and-dash. But before our appetizers arrived, we almost simultaneously spotted a woman seated next to me, with her purse on the floor, completely forgotten. We widened our eyes at each other, at the prospect of what we were potentially about to do.

"Should we?" I mouthed to Jenna.

"Let's take it to the bathroom and see if it's worth it," she in turn yelled into my ear. Jenna was always the ballsiest one.

I grabbed the purse and we went down to the bathroom.

The inside of a woman's purse is a good gauge of what type of person she is. In some ways, it's more intimate than an actual conversation. For example, a messy one means she probably doesn't change purses often, and prefers stability and monotony. Find a passport inside, she's likely spontaneous and flighty. Toothbrush or condoms, total slut. A mini umbrella always signifies responsibility.

This particular purse was nothing special. Wallet, tampons, gum. No coins at the bottom; she had changed her purse just for this occasion. In her wallet were the basics: IDs, credit cards, cash.

And receipts. Tons of them.

I started to backpedal. This was a woman who paid her own taxes. I assumed she was freelance. Probably, she had the mentality of "every penny counts." I knew because my dad is the receipt Nazi. Anytime he took a cab, ate at a restaurant, purchased an electronic item, he double-, triple-checked he had stored away the receipt.

"I think I saw a camera outside. What if she reports it missing and they see us on the video?" I wasn't about to admit I had gone soft. To my surprise, Jenna readily agreed. Maybe she was having second thoughts as well. Stealing from an actual human being was uncharted territory. We returned upstairs, purse in hand, and placed it back down on the floor next to my seat. Our food arrived shortly, we ate, paid for our meal, left a tip, and headed back to Jenna's.

After entering highschool, the trio slowly broke up. I met an older boy, Kevin, and spent most of my time with him and his pothead friends. My hobbies, although they still included shoplifting, gravitated more toward drug-related activities. Georgia continued being popular at UNIS, and Jenna eventually moved out to the West Coast with her parents. Sometimes I went shoplifting alone, sometimes with my best friend Dee. A few times I took Kevin on a stealing spree and got him anything he wanted. I never felt bad; I wasn't stealing from anyone personally, and besides, I was living by the phrase "Fuck the Man" at the time.

At age eighteen, I got caught for the first and only time. I should have known; the day was gloomy and raining, exactly the kind of weather right before bad things happen in movies. It was November, and I was stealing a bottle of perfume for Dee's birthday present. As I was about to walk out of the store, an employee called out to me.

"Excuse me, miss, please follow me."

My heart started to race. I began to feel dizzy. I followed the man to the back of the store, where they showed me a video of me putting the perfume in my purse. To this day, it makes me cringe in shame when recalling the image of myself crouched over, looking around to make sure no one was watching.

The police took me to the station, and after a few grueling hours, they drove me to Central Bookings, where I would spend the night. I was in disbelief. I had never been caught, and I always thought that if I had, it wouldn't come this far. Central Bookings was for crimes like selling drugs and tagging buildings, certainly not for little girls like me.

To get to the women's side of bookings, after taking your shoelaces, keys, and oddly enough, tampons, the guards walk you past a few rows of cells on the men's side. There were around fifteen men to a cell, some of them sitting in the back, others right up against the bars, yelling for things like water and food, or complaining about the temperature. They weren't talking to each other; they weren't really even talking to the guards. No one was paying attention to them; they were just yelling out into the atmosphere. As we walked past, I couldn't help but feel like we were walking through a zoo. It smelled disgusting, it was loud, and the air was chilly but thick. I didn't belong here.

The women's side was completely different. I was put in a cell with one other woman. There was a TV on the other side of the bars, easily visible from any angle within the cell. The toilet had a door; it was a door with no top or bottom, as if someone had cut off the two ends and just left the middle part. It was a door nonetheless. There was a mattress on the floor, and benches all around. It was cold, but it was still; there was nothing of the cold draft I felt on the men's side.

I sat down on a bench in the opposite corner from the other woman. She was black, and had braided red extensions in her hair. I noticed a nervous twitch, where occasionally when she blinked her eyes, she would blink them harder than was necessary.

After a few hours of silently watching a marathon of *The Fresh Prince of Bel-Air*, we were served our first meal: turkey sandwiches. I unwrapped the sandwich and put the packet of mayo to the side.

"You gonna use that mayo?" my co-inmate asked me. It was the first thing either one of us had said to the other.

"No, here." I walked up to her and handed her the mayo. *I thought black people were notorious for hating mayo*, I thought. My black friend Travis was always saying, "White people like mayo. Brothers don't fuck with that shit."

As if she were reading my mind, the next thing out of her mouth was "I must be the only black bitch who eat mayo. Whachu in here for?"

"Shoplifting," I answered as I sat on the bench next to her. "You?"

"Prostitution. My boyfriend about to be real fuckin' mad, too. I was drivin' his car tonight."

I didn't know how to reply. I had never met a hooker in real life. I had never even met a stripper.

"I called that nigga like five times and he still ain't pick up. This phone probably a blocked number or somethin'."

"How did they catch you?" I overexcitedly blurted out.

"Fuck, the police busted my club. I own two clubs uptown; they busted one of 'em last week. I got pulled over, next thing I know I'm here. I was tellin' my girl on the phone, why the fuck I'm here? I got pull over for speedin', now I'm in bookings? That ain't right."

I was confused why she was in jail. What did her club and speeding have to do with each other? She had said she was here for prostitution, but now it seemed like she just got pulled over. I was captivated.

"You must have crazy stories, huh?" I eagerly asked. We were going to be in here a long while. But things were starting to look up.

She told me she owned an after-hours club with her boy-friend. She and ten other girls hooked from there, but she was the main one. The club had been under investigation for a few months and finally got busted last week. Speeding in her boyfriend's car tonight, when she got pulled over and turned in her driver's license, it was expired. Having been arrested just last week for being at the club (she had ultimately been let go by saying she was just a patron), the police were quick to arrest her for driving with a suspended license. That's the story she told me, and I believed her. I would have believed it if she told me she had teleported here. This woman was the first woman I had ever met in the sex industry. She was my hero.

When she told me she had once posed in *Black Tail* maga-zine, I nearly fell off the bench. This was the least number of degrees there had ever been between me and porn.

"I look ratchety now but I clean up real nice, girl," she as-sured me.

"What are you talking about? You're so beautiful." I meant it.

We continued to talk the entire seventeen hours I was there, except for a small nap we attempted to take a few hours after eating our sandwiches. We exchanged information on where we got our nails done. I liked a marble nail design; she preferred a clean French. When we got cereal for breakfast, she gave me her milk. "That shit make me gassy as fuck," she told me.

By the time I left, I knew her whole life story. She knew nothing about me except for why I was there.

"It was really, really nice to meet you." I said to her when my parents' lawyer, Ezra, finally arrived. As the guard unlocked the gate for me, she looked at me with spite and did the twitchy thing when she blinked.

I left feeling incredibly inspired. "I just met the most amazing woman," I told Ezra.

"Let's not tell your mother," he answered.

As I walked out to appear in front of the judge, I realized I never even got my hero's name.

7
Art of the Blowbang

"I never said I wouldn't fuck anybody! I said I wouldn't fuck EVERYBODY! There's a FUCKING DIFFERENCE!"

Just something our lovely neighbors can typically hear coming from our balcony on any given night. It's not even embarrassing anymore, which is pretty shameful in itself. The problem with maintaining a relationship while pursuing a career in porn is that you have all the same problems as any other couple, but also a whole bunch of other bullshit added into the mix.

For the past three years, I'd been doing this series of movies called "Asa Akira Is Insatiable." It's difficult to bring these movies up without bragging about them; the first two alone have won about twenty awards. The premise is that I am, you got it, insatiable. Every movie escalates. My first anal and DP scenes were in the first one. In the second one are my first gangbang and double anal scenes. This next one, the third installment, I wanted to do the biggest blowbang I had ever done—eleven guys.

One of the greatest things about Toni is that he's been in the porn business 20 years. Twenty fucking years. That's longer than I've been having sex. It's longer than I've been giving blowjobs. It's pretty much longer than I've ever done anything, apart from just being alive. Because of this, he didn't suddenly flip a 180 and freak out over my work like some of the guys I had been with before. He understands it's my job, and as long as I stay respectful to him and follow a few of his rules, he doesn't really care.

The main one of those rules is no more gangbangs. I mean, I get it. Who wants their girlfriend to be the girl being passed between ten guys in an abandoned warehouse? We aren't swingers. Outside of our jobs, we don't fuck other people. We don't even have threesomes.

When I brought the idea of the blowbang up to him, Toni was cool with it. It's funny how everyone draws the line *somewhere*. In his mind, I wouldn't be fucking a group of guys, I would only be blowing them—and that was okay.

More than anything, Toni knew this movie was important to me. "Just don't fuck everybody and turn it into a gangbang. I know that's been your *thing*." This would be my first group scene since we'd been together.

"I won't! I won't fuck everyone. I promise. It's a blowbang."

I specifically chose these words so that I could hold my own in an argument later, that *everyone* and *anyone* were not the same thing. Which, ultimately, I suppose, just proves that I knew I was going to do something wrong all along. (I should add Toni is from Spain, and English is his second language. So I had that on my side as well. I don't fight fair, I know.)

Toni was right. I had a reputation for losing control in these type of scenes and turning them into all-out fuckfests. Something happens to me when I'm shooting a scene. Not just blowbangs and gangbangs, but any kind of scene. It never fails. I fall in love. Different from the emotional love I feel for Toni, but it's definitely some kind of chemical reaction in my brain that gets me into that happy place, where I feel passionate, desperate, vulnerable, but all in a good way. It's as if I'm in love with the *situation*, not the actual person I'm fucking. As odd as it sounds, porn has always been my dream. The thought of turning people on . . . doing something taboo . . . exposing myself for any perverts' eyes to see . . . the performance of it all just gets me going.

Once I got to set I knew what I had to do. I pulled the director aside, my friend Sam. "Listen. I promised Toni I wouldn't fuck everyone. I think I can get away with fucking three."

"Which ones do you want? I'll let them know ahead of time, and we'll tell our other eight friends no sex today."

"Pete for sure . . . His feelings will be hurt if I don't choose him. Ralph, too."

"Okay, and who else? Keep in mind that's two white guys."

"Right, right . . . Hooks is black. Let's do him."

Going into the scene, I didn't realize what I was in for, but once we started, I had to get with the program real quick. I had done two blowbangs before, as well as two gangbangs, so I was already familiar with the "cocks everywhere" aspect. The problem was that I had never done a scene in which I was fucking *some* of the guys, but not *all of the guys*. Silently, I swore to myself I'd never do a scene like this again.

As a kid, I always sucked at sports. It was just never my thing. My shitty hand-eye coordination, my reluctance to work on a team due to being an only child, my overall lack of physical elegance (I didn't even start walking until I was two years old), all contributed to my unpopularity in PE. Not to mention my now-ironic fear of balls coming at my face. I was always one of the last to be picked for a team. I knew I sucked.

Basically, this blowbang felt like PE class. And I was the team captain.

Hooks, you can fuck me. No, Eric. Pete, you're in. Eric, I already said you're not fucking me today. Snoop, I didn't choose you. Go on the other side.

In both blowbangs I had done previously, I ended up fucking everyone. Mostly because I was so turned on and just wanted to feel a dick in my pussy. But once I had fucked one, I wanted to keep going and fuck two, then three, and by the time you've fucked three, it's just bad manners to not let everyone play. This is secretly something I like about myself—I fantasize going down in history as a whore with a heart of gold.

The blowbang was a mixture of A-list male performers and just-blowbang guys. The blowbang guys are significantly cheaper, which is good when you need quantity, but in a (relatively) smaller blowbang like the one we were shooting, it's important to mix in some of the top guys to lead the way and ensure that the scene keeps moving—they're the "quality" in this equation.

As far as male-pornstar taxonomy goes, the A-list guys are at the very top. These are the guys who get to work with the best girls in the business; they have paid their dues and proven themselves to be good performers. I'd say there are only fifteen of them in the business, definitely no more than twenty. Some of them do features, but what every one of these guys must exceed at is Gonzo.

A-listers don't have issues getting their dick hard, keeping it hard, or popping on command. They are alpha males, always dominant, that can carry a scene and bring energy out of any girl. The ones nominated for "Male Performer of the Year" year after year at the AVN Awards.

Right under the A-list male talent would be the feature guys. Feature guys are the actors of porn. Best known for their acting skills and pretty looks, they aren't necessarily the best sex performers; sometimes they struggle to keep hard, and it never seems like the sex is the part they most look forward to. Considered to be the most "couple" friendly, they are in shape, tan, and clean-shaven—often, they are mainstream actors and models who lost their way and ended up in porn.

Below the feature boys, I'd say there's about 50 percent of the male talent pool in a big pile—these are the B- and C-listers. They are the "filler" male performers, who don't fit into any mold. You see them randomly on set, and work with them a few times throughout your career, but they aren't particularly memorable. The only time you hear their names is when they are dating someone more famous than themselves, or something crazy happens to them, like their dick breaks when a girls slams down on it too hard during reverse cowgirl.

Finally, at the very bottom are the blowbang guys. Also known as "mopes," they primarily do blowbangs and gangbangs. I'm talking about the kind of scenes where there is one girl and fifty-plus guys. The "creep" factor is abundantly in play here. Almost guaranteed to be chain smokers, they have prepaid phones and take the bus to location. It's not totally uncommon for them to be in and out of jail; nor is it uncommon for the director to lend them money to get their required monthly STD test. No one aspires to be a mope. It's just somewhere you end up.

Aside from the three guys I had chosen to fuck me, the guys for the blowbang scene that day had been told in advance that there would be no non-oral sex happening. But, of course—when they saw the chosen three fucking me, they assumed all bets were off. Imagine what it's like for a 105-pound girl to try to control eleven juiced-up guys. Now imagine that all those guys are on Viagra, and the girl is on the floor getting railed in her ass. It was a constant merry-go-round of subtly pushing, awkwardly crawling away, turning around to make sure the same three guys were still fucking me. Mind you, this is all while sucking eleven cocks. All while keeping everyone involved. Group scenes are not a selfish sport. There's no "i" in "blowbang." When the camera is rolling and that magic thing happens where every single guy is hard, you don't want to break the momentum and risk guys losing their wood by showing any kind of hostility. Especially the blowbang guys, who aren't as strong performers.

That day, I left the set patting myself on the back for somehow managing to get through the scene only fucking my three original guys, and all without hurting any feelings. I don't know which I was more proud of: my self-control, or my ability to coyly avoid fucking eight guys, all while keeping them happily engaged in the scene. Smiling all the way home, I ran a silent conversation in my head in which one Me referred to the other Me as a "master of the fine art of the blowbang."

A week later Sam called me. "Hey, dude. I'm editing. You want me to cut out the Snoop part, right?" I had no idea what she was talking about.

"Whachu mean?"

"The blowbang. The part where D.Snoop's fucking you. It's only a couple minutes long but he'd make our fourth guy. You only wanted three of our friends to have sex, correct?"

I was shocked. I was paying such close attention! I turned around every time a dick had entered me from behind to check who it was, I was sure of it.

"Snoop *fucked* me? Are you fucking joking me?" I couldn't help but laugh. That sneaky motherfucker! "Yah, cut it out, please. I can't believe he was fucking me and I didn't know!"

"Hey, you didn't know, it doesn't count!" I mean she was right. If she had never told me, I never would have known. This was too funny. How did he just slip in?

"It's the *Curious Case of D.Snoop.*" I joked.

"*The Haunting of Asa Akira.*" Sam caught on.

"*Snoop the Friendly Ghost.* Wait, no. *The Invisible Man* starring D.Snoop!" Bam, two for one.

"*Phantom of the Blowbang.*" And the winner is Sam.

I have to say, of all the slutty moments I've had in my life, this has to be top-three status. After getting off the phone, I contemplated telling Toni. Would he be mad about it?

At the end of the day, no matter the context, the person I want to share the events of my day with is Toni. There was already the whole misunderstanding about whether or not I told him I wouldn't fuck anyone at the blowbang. But it was too hilarious not to share, right? We were above fighting over trivial matters—after eighteen years in the business, one little slip of a dick couldn't possibly upset him. This was a legitimately hilarious story. I mean how many people can say, "I had no idea he fucked me!????"

If there were a category in *Guinness World Records* for "Sluttiest Thing to Accidentally Happen to a Woman," this would definitely be in the running.

I decided to chance it for the sake of a laugh.

He didn't think it was funny.

8
Girls

"Do you think I should tell Katie?" It was two in the afternoon and Mia was over. We were lying on opposite sides of the sofa in stained T-shirts and period underwear, passing back and forth a jar of peanut butter. A rerun of *Real Housewives* of someplace or another was on the TV but we didn't pay attention.

"Why not?" I replied. "What does she care if you fucked James or not?"

"She's trying to cut off her fuckbuddy she's in love with."

"Oh shit. Like you're in it together."

"Right. She's watching me."

Mia was my closest friend in L.A. She always had something going on; if it wasn't a cokehead boyfriend with babymama drama, it was her ex threatening to kill her from jail. An aspiring actress, she dated my ex-boyfriend after we had broken up. One day I had sent him a naked picture of myself, and she called me from his phone screaming. We've been best friends ever since.

"Omission isn't lying," I offered as I licked the spoon.

"She's gonna ask. Fuck it, I'm just gonna tell her I stayed in last night. My sex life is nobody's business. I'm gonna lie to her—just tell me I'm not a bad person for it."

I smiled. Mia could rob someone and I would probably justify it as the victim's fault. In fact, that had happened before.

"You're not a bad person for it."

"It's just he called me last night and was talking about fucking . . . And my pussy got so wet it was bubbling and dripped down to my ass without even being touched. His voice just makes me instantly wet."

"Like when people hear the word *cocaine* and instantly have to shit?" We laughed.

"Whatever. He limpdicked me half the night anyway."

James was a nightlife guy Mia had been seeing. He wasn't her boyfriend, partly because she already had one of those. He was a side piece she had caught feelings for. According to a self-help relationship book I once read, he was a classic "avoidant"—sends mixed signals, afraid to get too close, cold, insensitive, insecure. We were also suspicious he was on something, drug-wise, because his dick went limp all the time.

"It's so bizarre. I don't think I like him anymore anyway. Last night I shat on him a little while he was fucking my ass and I didn't care."

"If that's not a sign, I don't know what is. I've been with Toni for how long? And I don't want him to even know I shit, ever."

"Yah. I think I would've cared two fucks ago."

It was true. My friend Dave says it best: I'm anal about anal.

I never thought I'd be famous for my asshole. Really, I didn't. For as long as I can remember, I've been infatuated with porn. Growing up a Howard Stern fan, slutty girls were my heroes, somehow glorified in my mind. In movies and books, I was always drawn to the trashiest character in the story; the one who smokes cigarettes, is admittedly promiscuous, and almost always crazy in the most fascinating, brilliant way.

And yet, I never thought I'd be one of those girls. I never thought I'd have the guts.

Never say never.

I never thought I'd actually do porn. If anything, I thought I'd be a teen pregnancy case, divorced by twenty-one, second baby daddy by twenty-three. Possible herpes. I never thought the day would come I'd be labeled "Anal Queen" in every skin rag, or my asshole would win an award.

When I got into the business, I was adamant that I steer clear of anal sex. It was still a somewhat foreign concept to me, and I had this romanticized idea in my head that I should "save" my ass for the special guy who dealt with my crazy neurosis in real life. I thought it would make me relatively good wifey material, not *completely* used up. In fact, when I signed with my current agent Mark Spiegler, in my long proposal email on why he should represent me I told him one thing I would never do is anal sex on camera.

Hi Mark! This is Asa Akira. I was just curious to see if you are currently adding to your roster of girls . . .

My contract with GoldStar Modeling Agency ends on March 20th, in 12 days. After extensive research, and conversations w/various girls in the business, I've come to the conclusion you are the best.

I've heard you are very picky about the girls you take on, and pretty much everyone I have spoken to tells me the same thing: "you need to do anal."

I'll be honest with you, anal is not in my future. However, I just shot my first two interracial scenes for Jules
Jordan, in my own movie called *Invasian 4*. The movies
come out March 18th so after that, I plan on shooting
more!

Please let me know if you're interested in representing me.

> Thanks :)
> Asa

He loves showing this letter to everyone, mostly because I
went through a breakup and started shooting anal scenes two
weeks after I sent the email.

Anal sex is a strange thing in porn. My first month in, I
was under contract, shooting exclusively for a company called
Vouyer Media. One of the main directors there, Van, took
me to a Fourth of July barbecue at the house of the owner of
another company. This was my first time meeting Spiegler,
and he had brought some of the Spiegler Girls along with him.

"I did anal for Jules Jordan last week, and Mandingo fucked
my ass. I can't believe it fit!" one of them humble-bragged.

Not to be outdone, another girl exclaimed, "But have you
ever done *double* anal? I can pretty much fit anything back
there now."

"Donna put an entire double-ended dildo in my ass once
for Jay's *Deep Anal Drilling*."

What the hell are these girls bragging about? I thought.
Having a big asshole is a *good* thing? I'd never end up like that.

Alas, the curse. I had said it, even if silently, even if just to
myself. That word. *Never.*

I am totally like those other girls now. Toni hates it. "Just don't get like that about your pussy," he always reminds me. "I don't want you to stretch it all out."

Another thing I vowed upon starting to shoot anal scenes is that I would never get messy. I had heard horror stories: girls not cleaning out enough, shitting on guys on set. Not me. I'd be a pro from the start; no one was going to call me *that* girl.

Two years went by perfectly. I was known as a reliable anal performer; guys always told me fucking my ass was like fucking a pussy: a nice, warm hole, no mess. "I *never* get messy," I'd say. And that was it. The curse.

I was shooting a regular anal scene one day when I looked down at the cock entering my ass and saw a pool of red on the sheets right under the penetration. "Holy fuck! Cut, cut, cut! My ass is bleeding!" I yelled to everyone, no one in particular. There were five people on this small Gonzo set: me, the guy, the director, the photographer, and the production assistant, also known as the PA.

"You okay?" My male talent for the day was Tommy. In typical male pornstar fashion, he was juiced up on both steroids and Viagra. The Viagra I could tell from the flush in his face; his chest acne and body scent gave away the 'roids. It's a very specific smell—sour, and almost metallic.

I touched my ass with my hand, and to my horror, my fingers came back up covered in red. "I must be torn somewhere, right?" I asked, again to everyone, and no one in particular.

"Does it hurt, babe?" the director, Brian, asked me with his camera hanging on his shoulder.

"It doesn't . . . That's so weird. Frankie, come look at it for me." I called the PA over. The PA has possibly the worst job on set . . . which is to do all the crap no one else wants to do. Set up the lights, stand by with baby wipes, clean the cum off the furniture, and in this case, examine my asshole. I baby-wiped, bent over on the bed in doggy style, and put my ass in Frankie's face as everyone looked on.

"Anything?" I laid my cheek down on the sheets. What a pain in the ass this whole ordeal was, but oddly enough, not literally.

"I don't see anything; let me get the C-light." Brought in for close-up shots of the penetration, *C-light* is rumored to stand for *cunt-light*, but in all the years I've been in porn, no one has been able to confirm this for sure.

I spread my legs wider, put all my weight on my shoulders, and spread my asscheeks with both hands as my face smooshed deeper into the sheets. Frankie was bent over, one hand on his knee, the other holding the C-light; he squinted his eyes inches away from my asshole, which was gaping from being freshly fucked.

"What's it looking like?" Brian was getting restless. I could tell his mind was trying to gauge if he had time to go smoke a cigarette.

"I still don't see nothing."

"Fuck it, it doesn't hurt, lemme go rinse my butt out and let's keep going." I wasn't trying to waste anyone's time, including my own. I ran to the bathroom, enemaed, and came back to the set as Brian was finishing his cigarette and Frankie was putting a new sheet on the bed. We continued shooting; everything was fine. We switched from spoon into reverse cowgirl, where I was riding Tommy, but with my back toward him and my face toward the camera.

"Cut, it's bleeding again," Brian sighed as he put the camera down. "You sure you're okay? Let me see." I slid off Tommy, apologizing for the pool of red I left on and around his cock. I lay on my back and kicked my legs up and apart, ob-gyn style. Brian spread my asscheeks for me this time. "That's weird. I don't see anything. What's going on here?"

"Do you think I'm bleeding internally?" I started to enter panic mode. My ass had torn before, and it didn't bleed like this. What if my colon was bleeding? Or my intestines? Does that even happen? Where was my phone to WebMD the symptoms of bleeding internal organs during anal sex? I stood up and ran to the bathroom. Using my hands to hoist myself up onto the sink, I didn't give a fuck that I knocked over the expensive soap dispenser. I bent down in front of the mirror and looked at the reflection of my asshole from between my legs.

Nothing.

It was sparkling clean. I took a moment to appreciate my asshole. I took pride in it—some girls had extra skin hanging around; some you took one look at and knew immediately she was a seasoned anal pro. I exhaled and let my ass gape wider, in hopes to see inside. It looked pink and healthy, not bloody.

From the living room, Brian yelled to me. "You okay? What did you eat last night?"

What the fuck did he care what I ate last night, at a time like this. This could be cancer. What exactly were the symptoms of cancer, anyway? Had I caught an STD in my ass? Would I ever shoot porn again?

Just then I remembered my dinner. Fuck me fucking sideways. I had a fucking beet salad.

For a second, I wished my insides were actually bleeding. It would be less embarrassing. I took a moment on the sink, and stalled going out to tell everyone it was a false alarm, I'm fine, just ate beets last night. I'm supposed to be a fucking anal superstar. What an amateur move, not to mention disgusting; a man should never be able to tell what I ate last night from fucking my ass.

Slowly, I walked out. "So . . . I ate a beet salad last night. I'm sorry. I'll pay for everyone's kill fees, and reshoot this whenever you want for free." I bit my lip and waited for someone to tell me not to worry about it, it happens to the best of us.

Silence.

Then everyone burst out laughing. Like bent over, holding their stomachs, telling me to stop it, get out of here, no way, laughing.

I was mortified.

As Mia and I sat in silence while my thoughts continued to drift, the housewives on TV were arguing. One screamed "Get your finger out of my face!" as another declared "This isn't the place!"

It was always the same thing with these crazy bitches.

I loved it.

I had no siblings. I attended six different schools as a child. Possibly due to this, I never had many girlfriends. I would make one here and there, but having that core group of girl-friends, that *clique*, was something that never happened for me. When it comes down to it, I don't know if I would even *want* one; in all honesty, females, in groups, intimidate me. Nothing quiets me faster than a group of female strangers. All of a sudden I feel unsure, unworthy, insecure. *Is my outfit good enough? Am I too slutty to be likable? Do I know the right people?*

The women on this show wore thousand-dollar dresses to lunch, made judgments toward *everyone*, and name-dropped like their social lives depended on it. It was an elite female world, rich but classless, friendly but catty, that I would never be a part of. I was addicted to watching it.

"You know what's weird, too?" Mia broke the dead air.

"Hm."

"All Arabs smell the same. I didn't notice until I started messing with James. His scent reminds me of my dad's side of the family."

"Asians smell like garlic!" I jumped in excitedly. "And blacks smell the strongest!"

"Totally. Mexicans have a scent, too." Mia was part Mexican herself. "It's like, the spices they eat or something. Same with Indians."

"So weird, I never thought anyone else noticed," I said for probably the millionth time since I met Mia. She says we were sisters in a past life. I still haven't decided if I believe in that stuff, but I go with it.

"Twinssss," we chimed together in our period underwear.

I didn't realize I had such a strong sense of smell until I entered the porn business. In fact, for a long time, I had thought just the opposite; for sure, all those years of snorting Special K in highschool did some type of irreversible damage. While all my friends wisely switched nostrils every other line, I insisted it's better to fuck up one side of my nose completely, than to fuck up both sides mildly. It's been almost ten years since I've seen ketamine in any form, and even now, I wake up every morning with my left nostril stuffed up, needing to be blown. If the air is too dry, my nose will bleed, only on that side. I've convinced myself it's worth the fun I had.

I thought about the way Toni smells. Sometimes, when he's sleeping, I'll quietly go under the covers and just smell his dick. It's gross, I know; every time I do it, I think of the horror I'd face if he were to wake up. For a second, I'll try to make myself feel like I really did get caught. "Good morning, I'm just smelling your dick." How would I explain that? In reality I'd probably lie and tell him I saw a spider on his balls, or maybe I'd even go as far as to say I think I saw a lump.

The scent is specific to him, and when I inhale it, there's something comforting about it. It's not just his dick, although that's where it's the strongest—it's his whole being. There's nothing I love more than when we have a day off together, and he doesn't wear any deodorant. I just bury myself in his armpit and breathe.

As I sat there licking the peanut butter, I wondered if Toni could smell me. When I was sixteen, I dated a white boy who told me Asian girls smell different.

"I can only describe it as smelling like the color gray," he explained.

At the time, I didn't know what he was talking about; I just smiled and pretended to know what he was saying, which is how I spent most of my teen years around boys anyway. Now, over ten years and hundreds of girls later, I'm shocked at how observant he was at that young age. Or maybe he just fucked a lot of Asian chicks. I came to realize *gray* was the perfect way to describe it.

I grew up hardly knowing I was Asian. What I mean is, I was raised, for the most part, in the United States, and was never really that aware that my friends were of all different ethnicities and colors. In New York City, everyone is a minority. Downtown Manhattan is just a clusterfuck of every ethnicity; you have Chinatown, Little Italy, but also the West Village, and the projects. You go to the Upper West Side, everyone aside from Jews are a minority. Yet you go crosstown to the Upper East Side and it's nothing but WASPs. Go a little farther uptown from there and it's all Puerto Rican, Dominican, and black. Sprinkle Pakistanis, Asians, and Africans throughout and that's New York.

When I first started porn, I resented getting cast as the token Asian. Starring in *Oriental Babysitters 13: Anal Edition* was not what I had in mind when envisioning my career. One out of every three shoots was an "Asian" scene. I can't even tell you how many times I've covered my naked body in sushi, or played the role of a mail-order bride. "Masseuse" is something I can practically list on my résumé. Over time, I've come to embrace it. It's gotten me to where I am today, and it pretty much guarantees me work until the day I quit, since there is always a shortage of Asian girls in the business.

Mia broke my train of thought again. "I don't even know why I'm into him. He's forty-one. That's five years younger than my mom."

"Well, your mom is young . . ." I thought of how my own mother was almost sixty. I needed to have kids, soon. I didn't want to be an old mom.

"True. He's such a loser, though. What the fuck am I gonna do with that? It made me so mean to him last night. He's probably so confused."

"Eh, something about being mean makes the insecure guys stay more. It makes *me* stay, and I'm pretty much positive it says something about me that I'm not aware of."

"I was so bossy last night."

"Fuck, it's over. Once you're mean and they stay, it's game over! I can't respect that. And I'll just be mean until you leave."

"I think that's why I liked Colin so much." Colin was Mia's ex who turned out to be gay. Unknowingly dating a gay guy, another thing we had in common. "It kept me on my . . ."

"Best behavior!" we yelled at the same time.

Bitches are crazy, for sure, we both thought simultaneously.

Haiku

Squirted on the floor.

Now I have to clean it up

On my knees again.

9
Florida

Back then, before porn, I went by the name Akira. It was my stripping name, so when I was first asked to promote my club on the radio show, that was the name I used. By the time I was living in Florida and on the show as a regular, it was too late to request that people start using my real name. It's like Puff Daddy changing his name. *I don't care what you say; I'm never calling you Diddy.*

Having two names became my living nightmare. Every time I thought I got close to someone, there would be that moment they called me Akira—and I'd be snapped back to reality. *This person doesn't even know my name*, I'd overdramatically think. The worst was when my two worlds collided—half the people in the room would call me by one name, while the other half would call me another. I never quite knew how to introduce myself, so I just left it up to others to do it for me, undoubtedly making me seem cold. Not that there aren't perks to having a stage name. Your real name stays safe, untouched, un-google-able. It makes it easy to compartmentalize that era of your life, as well; for a year, I lived as another person. It's as if I didn't need to assume responsibility for any of my actions.

"Oh, that? That wasn't me. That was Akira. I would *never* get that wasted."

Without question, Florida is the trashiest state in North America. You hear a scandalous story about a woman and her daughter getting into porn together, and you just know it's happening in Florida. A man with a mullet shoots an innocent bystander because he can't take a doggy bag home at an all-you-can-eat buffet—you don't even have to ask! It's bound to be a story from Florida. I'll often join in on conversations mocking Floridians and their white trash ways, and forget I myself spent an entire year out of my life living there.

"It's awful," I'll remark. "I just stop listening after 'I'm from Florida.'"

It's true. Being from New York, where even being born in Staten Island is almost too embarrassing to confess, admitting I resided in Tampa is not something that comes easily to me. The radio show had discovered me at the "gentleman's lounge" I was working at in the city, and moved me down to the Sunshine State to start a solo-girl website endorsed by the show. In addition, I went on the air two or three times a week as the "Show Whore." I should specify that the term *whore* wasn't used literally. It was my first job in media, and immediately I knew I loved it.

Running my website was Hank. Hank was a millionaire. Of course, he wasn't the first one I had met, but he was the first one in *Florida* that I knew. Being a millionaire in Florida is much different than being a regular one; it's much flashier, much trashier. Very *new money*. Hank had started a porn website, back when porn sites had just started to dominate the Internet. The site is still running to this day, but it's way past its heyday; by the time I met him, he owned several strip-clubs and had invested in random businesses, the radio show being one. By first impression, you wouldn't think Hank was a successful businessman. He had the vibe of an entertainer, always "on." His favorite joke was to take the skin of his balls out through the fly of his pants, walk around pulling on it, innocently offering around, "Gum? Does anyone want some gum?"

For the year I was in Florida, I lived in the guest house of Hank's mansion, in which he resided with his wife and two kids, ages sixteen and two. Forties, blue eyes, balding, what Hank lacked in conventional good looks, he made up for with charm and charisma. In his own goofy way, Hank could be considered cute; but Laura was the real beauty in the relationship. In her thirties, she was classically beautiful. Not in the cheap, offensive way so common to the state. Her Native American genes shone through, and the only thing fake about her were her boobs; everything else, including her personality, was very real. To this day, she is probably the most grounded person I've met.

Complete with a movie theater, saltwater pool, and library, their place was extravagant in that faux-marble paint, Florida way. In the main entrance was an oversize Elvis mannequin. Elvis was Hank's idol; a popular nighttime activity in the mansion was to take Ambien and purchase Elvis memorabilia on eBay. Neither I nor Hank would remember in the morning, and we'd laugh listening to Laura inform us we had spent thirty thousand dollars on a shirt once worn by the King of Rock himself.

"No way. I just remember making nachos . . . then we went to bed!" Hank would smile while he said this, knowing in the back of his mind what we had done.

"Not only did you leave open cans of beans everywhere, Akira, there are four spoons in the dishwasher covered in peanut butter."

Guilty. Around that time, I was carrying a jar of peanut butter with me everywhere I went. It was before my metabolism turned on me, when I could do things like order a whole pizza just for myself without thinking about how it would affect my love handles. If only I had known then what the future had in store for me; I would have spent all my time eating high-carb foods, instead of doing drugs and having sex.

I don't recall exactly when the three of us became a couple, or how it was initiated. It was in my OxyContin phase, so the timeline is a bit blurred. It's hard to make out whether we had all fucked first, or if I fucked Hank alone first, or if they had started calling me their girlfriend before anyone had sex. The latter sounds about accurate; I believe they had started calling me their "girlfriend" as a joke, and reality just gradually started to imitate that.

Before I paint a picture of some freaky, year-long sexual experiment, I should mention that Hank and Laura weren't swingers. I try not to judge, but it would be a lie to say swingers aren't weird fucking people. They have an air of desperateness to them that I can't quite get with. The one time I went to a swingers party was by accident; my date had told me we were going to a party, and I was there for over an hour before I realized exactly what kind of party it was. "Are you okay?" he kept asking me, and I had no idea why—until, that is, some vaguely recognizable child actor of the eighties and his wife came swimming up to me, rolling on Ecstasy and talking about the girl they fucked last night.

Sex was probably about the third-biggest factor in the relationship of Hank, Laura, and myself. Looking back, the dynamic was certainly strange. I was in love with both of them. We didn't necessarily fuck every night. Sometimes I would sleep in bed with them; sometimes I would sleep alone. If one was out of town, I'd sleep in bed with the other. There were mornings I'd be in bed with Hank, and the sixteen-year-old daughter, Brynn, would come in and join us for a morning chat in the bedroom. It was more normal than it sounds.

Often at night, I'd sneak into the master bedroom for some fun, after the kids went to sleep. We'd fuck like animals, and then sit around and talk for hours. Hank and I would always be pilled up by then, but Laura hardly partied. Hank would take out his guitar and play his favorite Elvis song as Laura and I lay cuddling.

I became extremely close with Brynn. During the day, Hank would go to work. Sometimes I had to go with him, but for the majority of the week I was free during the day. Laura always had house stuff to do; she was endlessly busy. It was during that time I realized no job is busier than that of a mom. There's always something to be done, and a never-ending list of errands, and when you get home, you're still working. It should be a paying gig.

"Akira! Come to the main house!" Brynn would yell into the guesthouse. I'd come downstairs, outside, we'd walk across the pool, and into the main house. Bri wasn't allowed to have a boyfriend yet, but we'd talk about the boys she liked. She would get home from school right around the time I woke up, and we'd then go to the mall, watch TV, do each other's makeup, swim in the pool . . . regular teenager stuff. I was playing a sixteen-year-old by day, sisterwife by night.

Hank always boasted that he had never fought with Laura, and she supported this statement. In the time I spent with them, I never saw them get upset with each other. It wasn't like they bottled their feelings up, or internalized any anger—they simply didn't disagree on much, and if they did, they were genuinely okay with agreeing to disagree. I still haven't figured out if it's the healthiest or unhealthiest thing I've ever seen.

"I have a big announcement," Hank slurred to us one night after we had attended a birthday party. Already a few pills in, we were all feeling good—even Laura, since her mom was staying the night with the baby. "Meet in the hot tub in ten minutes."

Laura and I giggled as we watched Hank come in and out of the kitchen, collecting candles and such from all around the house for our "meeting."

Once in the hot tub, Laura and I pawed at each other's bodies.

"Sit still for one second, guys, so I can make my announcement."

"There's actually an announcement?" I laughed. I thought he was just saying that to get us all in the hot tub.

"The floor is all yours," Laura said, and winked at me as she sat back into another nook in the tub.

With his eyes closed and his hands up like an orchestra conductor, he declared, "Here's my announcement. I love you guys."

Pause.

"That's it?" Laura burst out laughing.

Without trying to hide his disappointment, Hank came to sit between us, and put his arms around us. "I mean it, you guys. I'm not joking. I swear, I love you both."

He was nearing tears. The pills do that sometimes, escalate emotions. And it's contagious. It was spreading to me, too, fast.

"Wait, wait. I love you, too. Both of you. I'm so happy to be with you guys." Now I started to cry. I was now officially a passenger on this emotional roller coaster. I started thinking about my life, and how I ended up here, in this strange ménage à trois. It wasn't conventional, but it worked. I was happy. I felt close to them, and a *part* of something.

"I think my babysitter raped me when I was young," I started confessing.

I had never said these words out loud before. "I have no real reason to think it, and no way to prove it."

Laura swam over to the other side of me, and ran her fingers through my wet hair.

"I had a male babysitter when I was two or three. I slept in a toddler bed, and I remember we had this joke, where he'd crawl into my bed with me. I thought it was the funniest fucking thing, a grown-ass man in my toddler bed."

Hank held my hand.

"I loved him. Then one day, he was just gone. I asked my parents where he went, and my mom just told me, 'Just because we don't like him anymore, it doesn't mean you can't like him.' That's a weird fucking answer, right? Even back then it felt cryptic and weird."

Hank was crying with me. Laura was holding me.

"This sounds so fucking cliché and I hate it, but the worst part is—I'm pretty sure I fucking liked it! When I think of him, nothing but positive feelings come up. I don't feel scared, or resentful; If anything, it makes me smile."

I looked up through my tears at both of them. They were hanging on to me, tightly.

"No one has ever shown me love like this before." It probably wasn't the truth, but it felt like the right kind of moment to say something like this. "I'm so grateful to have you in my life." That part was undoubtedly true.

We sat there in the hot tub, the three of us crying, for what seemed in OxyContin-time like hours. I felt so emotionally charged, saying these words I had never been able to say out loud before. Naked, crying, talking about my suspicion of a childhood rape that I had no valid reason to back it up with, I was in the most vulnerable state a person could be in.

Hank looked me in the eyes.

"We love you, Akira."

Shit Pornstars Say

"Don't cum in my eye."

Whatever context it's said in—whether it be a joke, threat, or gentle warning—this phrase is a curse. The moment these words are uttered, you've just guaranteed yourself sperm in your eyeball.

Sometimes it's the male performer. He does it on purpose; he's having a bad day, he woke up to his girlfriend yelling at him, he hits traffic on the way to the set, and finally, upon getting out of the car after an hour and a half, he finds out he is working with a girl he has no chemistry with. The girl gives him a list of a million things he cannot do to her, starting with "don't touch my hair," and ending with "don't cum in my eye." He struggles through the scene, needing to cut every few minutes to get his dick back up. Finally, when the director gives him the nod, signaling him to cum, he projects his rage into his pop shot, and bam. "Accidentally" cums right on her cornea.

More often, though, the male talent has little control of exactly where his pop goes. "Face" is a pretty general area, and the eyes are a big part of said area. It happens.

* * *

"Where are the baby wipes?"

What the baby wipe industry doesn't know (or do they?) is that mothers of newborns are not the ones keeping them in business. It's sluts. It's whores. It's pornstars. In porn, we use baby wipes for *everything*.

Pee. "Where are the baby wipes?" Dirty feet. "Where are the baby wipes?" Dusty furniture. "Where are the baby wipes?" It's hot in here. "Where are the baby wipes?" (Apply cold baby wipe to nape of neck.)

Whenever I'm on a non-porno set, like say a music video, or an independent movie, I have to constantly remind myself not to ask for baby wipes. It's like a huge neon sign with an arrow pointing down to me, saying in all caps, "SEX WORKER."

If a girl has baby wipes in her house, but no baby—I'd say she will most likely be down to let you put it in her ass.

"I have to clean my ass."

It seems like a big portion of my life is spent cleaning my ass.

"I can't go out tonight, I have to clean my ass." Or "Let me call you right back—I'm cleaning my ass."

Of course, everyone has their own system, but I like to prep for my anal scene a day in advance. I wake up in the morning, work out, then start the process. The sooner in the day I can do it, the better.

The process is simple. I take an enema bag, fill it up with water, feed it into my ass through a tube, let it out, repeat.

I get paid almost a thousand dollars extra when a scene entails anal, as opposed to just vaginal. When I first started shooting anal scenes, it didn't seem fair . . . a hole is a hole, and one isn't worth much more than the other.

But as I sit here, refilling the enema bag over and over while browsing the Internet, I realize . . . They're not paying me extra 'cause it's my asshole. The extra grand is for the prep that goes into it.

"I have cancer."

Beautiful, with the kind of face that comes by porn no more than once every few years, Raven joined Spiegler's roster of girls a couple of years after myself. Seemingly normal, there was nothing offensive about her—a country girl, with two little kids and a steady boyfriend.

Less than a year after she signed with Spiegler, she announced she had cancer. It's completely horrible, but my first instinct was:

"It's a lie."

I expressed my thoughts to Spiegler and Dana, and they agreed with me. Cancer was a common subject when it came to liars in porn, and the business was full of them. Someone ought to do a research on women in porn—we have an astounding amount of pathological liars being exposed every day. So six months later, when Raven started to post pictures online of her bald self wig-shopping, we all felt bad. I called Spiegler telling him not to tell anyone what I had said.

Months went by, and Raven got worse. People who had seen her said she had dropped a dramatic amount of weight, and her skin had gotten grayish. Her boyfriend tweeted the progress of her disease, stating Raven had gotten too sick to respond to her fans on the site. Eventually, she became too weak to walk and needed to be physically carried in and out of her wheelchair when leaving her home. Which was ironic, because after her boyfriend quit his job to take care of her two children, Raven made money by webcamming with fans, and escorting.

Almost a year went by, when Raven switched to an all-vegan diet and started drinking alkaline water, and suddenly, miraculously, was cured. Her doctors informed her that her body was free of cancer. Around this time, someone on Twitter asked her why, if she had lost all the hair on her head, did she still have eyebrows. A few days later, she posted a picture of herself with no eyebrows.

Just as suddenly as she was cured, her boyfriend left her, deleted all of the cancer-related tweets, and posted a final tweet, that his girlfriend was a liar.

"Do you think . . . ?" I carefully, yet excitedly questioned Dana.

"We called that shit first," Dana said, smiling.

10
No Sex in the Champagne Room

"Assume the position, ma'am."

Pause.

"And I use the word *assume*, because I *assume*—"

Pause.

"—that you've been in this position before."

The crowd of two-hundred-plus horny ladies went wild.

This was my first encounter at a male stripclub. My thoughts on such a place had always been simple: Male strippers are gross.

We were there for Anita's birthday. My friend Ellie's cousin's ex-husband owned the club, so she had hooked it up for us. We thought the experience would be fun in a totally ironic way—like, "Ha-ha, look at these Fabio dudes dancing! What losers!"

We were wrong. These men were hot as fuck.

Onstage, "Nico"—dressed in stripper police gear, complete with Ray-Ban sunglasses and an artificial-hormone-fed figure—was standing behind a woman he had bent over the chair. Laughing, blushing from a combination of embarrassment and drunkenness, the woman would be somebody's wife tomorrow. Tonight, though, her girlfriends had signed her up to simulate sex acts onstage with a man wearing a thong under his cop uniform.

As the theme from the show *Cops* played, Nico tore his uniform off and danced around the stage. The crowd cheered on as he did backflips in nothing but shoes and a small piece of cloth covering his dick and asshole. A frumpy woman, presumably an employee, came onstage to escort the bachelorette off as more Nico-looking men, only dressed in tearaway prison outfits, joined in on the act.

Ellie had gotten us a booth right up front, so we could enjoy the show with the best view in the house. But the real show was behind us.

Women yelling, banging on the tables, jumping up and down on the chairs. Out of context, you would have thought we were monkeys in a zoo at feeding time.

If I were a man working at this club, I would be terrified of women.

I mean we were frightening.

The show had opened with six shirtless men dancing to 50 Cent's "In da Club." The lights beamed off their oiled muscles, making the women scream so loud I thought it was a tape recording to get the crowd going. I had never heard noises like that in my life.

I was screaming, too.

Some of them danced better than me. Scratch that. All of them danced better than me. A couple of them even did pole tricks, which I don't do at all. I wondered how much they make. Had any of them done gay porn? I wondered if they were all just flaming homosexuals outside of this club. These men were too aesthetically pleasing to be straight. Gay retail clerk by day, women's sex object by night? Straight for pay?

A few men, for their solo shows, danced to the same songs I used to dance to when I was stripping. I wonder if the same things ran through their heads while they dance. *Why am I here? How many more minutes until my shift is over?* Did they hate this job as much as I had?

It's not that I didn't enjoy dancing. It's not even that I didn't enjoy the men I was dancing for. In fact, once I was onstage, once I was interacting with the crowd, once I was giving lapdances, I enjoyed myself. It's the late hours, the dirty clubs, the million cigarettes I ended up smoking in the dressing room . . . Too tired to do anything during the day, not wanting to eat too much before going naked in front of hundreds of men . . . Unrolling the filthy dollar bills thrown at me before finally washing all the grime off my body in the shower at 5 a.m.

My saving grace was Maury, the closest thing I've ever had to a sugar daddy. I had been dancing for a few months at the Hustler Club, and Maury was a known big spender.

"If he likes you, he'll take you to the champagne room every night. You don't even have to be dirty." The host winked. He took my hand and walked me over to an elevated VIP table.

"Come sit with us!" Maury shouted over the music. There were already a good five or six girls sitting with him, all laughing, all beautiful. It seemed almost cartoonish, these long-legged, Jessica Rabbit–looking women surrounding this fat, gray-haired Jewish man. They had the desperate-ness of wanting cash written across their faces, but they all seemed to be familiar with and even to enjoy Maury's company. The Hustler Club in New York City is somewhat different from the average titty bar across Middle America; it's a "gentleman's lounge," a whole other breed of stripclubs. The ceilings are high, there are three stages, and the seats are clean, free of holes and stains. There's a cigar lounge upstairs on the roof, which is lit by tea lights and looks out over the Hudson River. The women are dressed in long gowns instead of bikinis, and one-dollar bills are not crumpled up and thrown onstage. Money is made not on the stage, but in private dances, and mostly in the Champagne Room.

"Hi, Maury. I've heard so many good things about you from all of the girls. I'm Akira." That was the stage name I used back then.

We had some small talk before he eventually signaled the host back over, telling him he wanted to take me to the Champagne Room. At the words "Champagne Room," the energy of the group shifted. Every girl sitting with us sat up a little taller, paid attention a little closer.

"I'm gonna go with Akira tonight," he said as each face fell.

Maury paid the host with cash. Four hundred dollars for the club, the "hourly room fee," and an additional six hundred dollars for me.

Once we were alone in the room, I didn't know what to expect. Some guys, I had to hint at a blowjob to get in here. Of course, once we got into the room, I would spend the next hour putting off the promised oral sex, instead just giving a lapdance that lasted too long for both of us. With some guys, I turned into their therapist; they'd complain to me about their wives, girlfriends, mistresses, and I just became a helping ear. Some guys just wanted company while they snorted coke for an hour, cutting their lines with their corporate credit cards.

This wasn't the case with Maury. I undressed, danced a little bit for him, and then we talked about random things while chain smoking, me naked, him fully clothed. I did come to find out he was an Orthodox Jew, unhappily married with two kids, and he owned a successful business in the city. For the most part, though, our conversation was that of two friends, just shooting the shit. Maury didn't drink; I didn't, either. I was on Oxys, but at the time he didn't know that.

We ended up exchanging numbers that night before we left the Champagne Room and went home separately, both feeling we had made a new friend.

From that point on, any night Maury was at Hustler, which we jokingly referred to as "H," I was there, too. I lived two blocks away from the club, and he would text me as soon as he arrived. I'd throw on some makeup, pop an Oxy, and head over to the club in my pajamas. Some nights I would head up to the locker room to change into my stripperwear; some nights I didn't even bother. He always, always took me to the Champagne Room.

More often than not, Maury would hire another girl to come into the room with us. There was a roster of ten or so girls that he liked. Sometimes, if it was a girl I was attracted to, he'd watch us fuck. The hottest girl was Jacqueline. She was a Puerto Rican Barbie doll. She got too drunk sometimes, but Maury didn't mind. It was part of her charm. Many nights, Maury would take me out from the club, paying me my hourly Champagne Room fee, to go eat, hang out at his office, or even go to another stripclub. We'd pick up my two best girlfriends, Dee and Gianna, on the way to wherever we were going. Seven a.m. would roll around, and he would drop us off at our homes and head straight to work, or home for a nap. I never knew what he told his wife. Maury was truly my friend; only, he paid me.

Eventually, Maury made a proposal. We would stop with the Champagne Room business and he would pay for all my bills and give me an allowance—for the exchange of my company a few times a week. It wasn't much different from what I had already been doing; it just meant Maury wouldn't have to pay the club their fee. I agreed.

Shortly after the agreement, Maury took me and Jacqueline on a business trip to Florida.

We stayed at the Ritz-Carlton, and Maury had gotten Jacqueline and me a room to share, and he had a suite next to us. Jacqueline and I had become close, so this was no problem. Our first full day there, Maury had to work, so Jacqueline and I went down to the pool. That night, we went out to a nice dinner and ended the night back at the hotel, Maury in his room, us in ours.

The next day, Maury was free. We went on a shopping spree, where we got thousands of dollars' worth of clothing. Maury was happy to see us happy.

"By the way, I hired some girls for tonight if you guys wanna join." We were eating lunch after our shopping spree when Maury dropped this on us.

"Actually, my friend Toby lives here, and he's been hitting me up. I was hoping we could meet up with him."

So it was settled. Maury would see the escorts that night, and Jacqueline and I would go out with Toby.

The night with Toby is a blur, but I remember enough to know it was one of those perfect nights out that only happen when you're twenty-one, old enough to be an adult but young enough to be free of responsibility. We were all fucked-up, but no one went accidentally overboard. I remember him and his three friends coming to get us. I remember popping a couple of Oxys before we left. I remember doing lines of coke throughout the night. We hit a few clubs, getting into each one for free because of our outfits. We definitely went skinny-dipping at the beach. I vaguely remember the boys dropping us off at the hotel, and making out with Toby before I got out of the car.

Jacqueline and I woke up the next afternoon wearing the boys' collared shirts. Maury was sitting at the edge of my bed.

"I took the liberty of going through your camera," he said sadly.

I looked over at Jacqueline, who I could tell was trying to put the pieces of the night together.

"Oh, cool," I answered. It was weird he went through our stuff. For half a second I started to get offended, but then quickly decided I was too tired to try to care. "How was your night?" I asked.

"It was good. You guys look like you had fun." Maury's voice made me feel guilty for having fun.

"I don't even remember what we did last night." It wasn't totally true, but somehow I thought it would make him feel less left out.

We ordered breakfast to the room, and Maury was quiet. We went out to drive around Miami, and he was quiet all day. At one point his wife called. This was the first time he answered her call in front of me.

"Hey . . . Nothing, just work. How are the kids? Good. I'll call you tomorrow." He almost hung up, when he blurted,

"Wait—I miss you." Pause. She didn't say anything back. He hung up.

We went back to the hotel, and I started to roll a joint.

"Maury—you wanna smoke?" I knew his answer would be no.

To my surprise, he answered, "Sure."

Jacqueline and I looked at each other. Maury had never done any type of drug before. Not that I consider weed a drug, but he had never been high.

The best thing about getting someone high for the first time is that it takes you back to the time *you* got high for the first time. All the new surreal sensations, the silly ideas, the finding everything hilarious . . . It's contagious. There's a great deal of my early teen years that I don't remember, but the first time I got high is one memory that plays as vividly as one that happened yesterday. I was in Central Park with my girlfriend Jenna and four boys. The first image I saw high was a man sitting on the park bench reading a newspaper. It was summertime, so he was wearing no shirt; his newspaper covered his shorts, and it made him look like a naked man reading the newspaper in Central Park. After laughing for what could have been five seconds or five hours, Jenna and I left the boys to go to FAO Schwarz. We played with the toys, lay among the stuffed animals, and walked around in a hysterical daze until we ultimately got thrown out for eating the candy out of the tubs in the candy store. We went back to Jenna's house with one mission: Find more weed.

As we passed our third joint around, Jacqueline and I decided to put makeup on Maury. I took out a skirt and draped it around his head like a turban. We all fell to the floor laughing.

We ordered room service and the boy who brought our food joined us briefly, taking pictures of "the strippers" to send to his friends.

From that day forward, Maury was hooked. He started smoking before he went to the office, and didn't stop until it was time to go home at night. He went to H less and less, and eventually even stopped seeing me. He told me him and his wife had started smoking together, and even had sex for the first time in over a year.

I still talk to Maury occasionally, and he's always high. He sounds like a different person; I didn't realize it at the time, but Maury was depressed when I met him. He doesn't go to stripclubs anymore, doesn't see girls anymore. He never asks me to hang out.

That makes me happy.

To the left of me, as the nearly naked men danced onstage, Anita was stuffing a dollar down the crotch of a waiter dressed in black slacks and a bow tie. No shirt.

"C'mon, baby, you can reach further down than that!" he yelled over the noise of the music and women.

She laughed.

In an environment like this, women are much more aggressive than men. A good number of us extended our arms onto the stage to cop a feel. Any piece of flesh would do—a thigh, a bicep, upper left shoulder, whatever. Upon getting their cocks grabbed, the strippers only smiled and gave them the side-to-side finger wave, as if to say "nuh-uh-uh, silly." If men acted this way at a female stripclub, they'd be thrown out immediately—possibly even arrested.

Maybe because I had already been DP'd earlier that day, maybe because I was already used to seeing men naked on a daily basis; maybe because I myself was objectified so often, or maybe because I was just more reserved in general, I didn't touch any of the men. How strange it felt to be on this side of the stage, on this side of the gender dynamic.

It reminded me of a documentary I saw about male escorts in Japan. Their clients, the women, would come back to their club night after night, patiently waiting as they serviced other women ahead of them. They would bring them extravagant gifts, buy expensive bottles of champagne, shower them with any amount of money they asked—all for nothing but their companionship.

The twist was, these women were hookers.

They would work all day, have sex with men for money, go to the club at night, and spend it all on their male escort of choice. The dirty side of the circle of life.

A girl from our group, Angie, waved a dollar while jumping up and down.

"Come here! Come over here!"

It made me cringe. It made me hate her. I resented that, the whole *Come over here, I have a WHOLE DOLLAR! Now show me what you'll do to deserve it.*

It's offensive. I hated when men had that attitude when I was dancing.

Right then, "Christian" came on the stage. Upon his reveal, several woman got up from their seats and rushed the stage. Rightfully so—this mixed boy, he was beautiful. Probably half black and half white, he had light brown skin and what looked, from below the stage, like hazel green eyes. His body was ripped. Big lips, and a face that seemed boyish and manly all at once. Anita and I looked at each other with matching expressions.

"Whoa."

We pushed and shoved our way to the front of the stage, where other women had just pushed and shoved their way ahead of us a moment ago. Anita grabbed my hand.

"That boy is fucking beautiful."

I nodded my head yes without taking my eyes off him.

He was obviously the crowd favorite. When he finally took his clothes off, I swear the room shook from the noise.

He came toward us, and when he bent down onto his knees and rolled his abs with a smile, Anita slipped a dollar into his G-string. He smiled, in a way that made me rethink everything I was feeling a second ago. If he could smile like this, so genuinely, so convincingly, maybe I could, too.

I brushed his leg as he crawled away.

Haiku

Penis in my throat!

If I had a gag reflex

. . . I could eat way more.

11
Glory

Whenever I fly, I try to get to the airport at the very last minute that I can. The longer I'm there, the more crap food I eat. Raised by health nuts, I can count on one hand the times I was "treated" to dinner at McDonald's as a child. Junk food was never a part of my palette, let alone on the list of things I allow myself to eat now that I have a job that requires me to be naked most of the time. Yet, somehow, when I'm in an airport, all bets are off. It might be the chemical scents the food chains release into the air; or possibly just the sheer boredom of being stuck in an airport with an iPod full of music I don't feel like hearing, and an iPad full of eBooks I don't feel like reading. Whatever the reason, a delayed flight is my diet's worst enemy.

This was the case that morning. After roaming the airport, passing the Cinnabon stand for the fifth time, I finally sat down at the gate.

Day after Thanksgiving, and I was on my way to New Hampshire for a store signing.

Winter holidays are always the worst time to travel, and it's a cliché in itself to even complain about it. JFK was particularly crowded that day, even for this time of year, and I took the first open seat I saw. I heard an overhead announcement saying we wouldn't be boarding for another two hours, but the Pizza Hut Express and Häagen-Dazs ice cream cone I just ate, along with the leftovers my mom fed me before I left, had me too full to scavenge any further.

The seat I chose was next to a ponytailed man-boy dressed in a Metallica T-shirt and some dirty black jeans. I guessed he was about twenty.

"You going to Rochester?" I turned to see who was talking to me. Strangers make me nervous, but this kid seemed innocent enough.

"No." I answered. ". . . New Hampshire. Flight's delayed."

"Our flight was d-delayed too. W-w-w-we're supposed to be boarding in ten minutes, but they've been telling us that for the p-past three hours. What can I say? That's JFK." He was stuttering, like his mouth was moving too fast for his brain. This probably meant he knew who I was, which was good. Immediately, I felt like we had something in common, a dirty secret. Like in a "Pervs unite" kind of way. It put me at ease.

"I'm Rob." He stuck his hand out for me to shake it. I took it.

"I'm Asa. Nice to meet you."

We continued a bit more of the delayed-flight-talk before I took out my iPad and he went back to playing his Nintendo DS. His boarding zone was called not much later. He took a second to gather his things and I told him to "have a nice flight."

The next ten seconds happened in slow motion.

Rob stood up and crossed in front of me. As he walked around behind my seat, he reached down, past my face, over my shoulder, down my chest, and grabbed my tit. Then he gave it a firm squeeze.

And then he ran away.

A second later, I began to register what had happened. I looked around me to see if anyone had noticed. Was this really happening? Is this real life? Am I being punished for all those rape jokes I made on Twitter? After freezing for ten seconds or so, I picked up my coat and purse and ran after him. Just like in a nightmare, I felt like I was watching all of this happen to myself, and my reaction to everything was always two seconds delayed. The airport was crowded, and by the time I was up and running, he was nowhere to be seen. I went up to the gate and told the flight attendant. "Some idiot just grabbed my breast. He's going to be boarding this plane." Tears were starting to form in my eyes, and my voice was shaking. I wanted to control myself so badly, but I physically couldn't. I felt violated, like in that dream where someone opens the door to the public bathroom just as I'm crouched over, one leg up on the toilet seat, phone clenched between my teeth, changing my tampon.

The most fucked-up part about someone grabbing my tit like that was that I didn't react how I wanted to. Instead of punching him, slapping him, or at least telling him off in an intellectual manner, I froze, cried, and tattled.

I ended up missing my flight and taking the next one so that I could give a statement to the police. When I did finally land in New Hampshire, I barely had time to take a nap before a car came to pick me up for my signing. "The craziest thing just happened to me," I explained to the store employee on the drive over.

We got to the store and it turned out it was a family-owned business. Running it was a mother-son team, Abigail and Mike. I had an hour before the store officially opened, so I had Mike give me a tour. Upstairs was where all the videos, lingerie, stripper shoes, and sex toys were sold.

"I don't know if you want to see the downstairs," Mike laughed.

"Why wouldn't I?" Whatever was downstairs, it sounded promising already. If anything, the boy had challenged me.

Mike looked up at his mom. "Can I?" he asked, seeming boyish all of a sudden, despite his actual late-twenties age.

Mom said okay and we headed down the uneven wooden steps. The farther down we went, the colder it got. I felt like the kids from the Narnia series, walking through a dark closet to unveil a secret. A security guard let us through a black curtain at the bottom of the stairs.

What it opened to was a row of booths, some with curtains open, some closed. Each of them was playing a porno on a small TV screen. They were all empty.

"Come, look." Mike led the way into a booth. A gay movie that couldn't have been filmed later than the eighties was playing in this one. I followed Mike's gaze under the TV screen, and to my amazement, there it was: a single, perfectly round gloryhole, all alone in the middle of the wall.

"Do they all have it?" My voice was projecting about four notches too loud and a whole pitch higher than usual.

"Yup."

I ran into the next one. And the next one. And the next one. They were all connected by the same-sized holes, with swinging sheets of wood to cover them for when they weren't desired.

"Is this legal?" My voice was still too loud. Mike laughed.

"Nah, but we say it's for ventilation." He made the air quotes with his hands.

I took out my phone and handed it to Mike. "Quick, take a picture of me through the gloryhole."

When we finally went back upstairs, it was time for the store to open. Less than twenty-four hours ago I had been molested for the first time in my adult life, but all I could think about was the gloryholes. Maybe it was true what they said, before light comes darkness. I had never seen one in real life before; I had never even seen one on TV. It was something I had been hearing about. I didn't want to sign autographs. I wanted to go look at the gloryholes again.

I tried to incorporate the mystical holes into every conversation I had. "Nice to meet you. Oh I *loved* making this movie. Have you ever seen a real-life gloryhole??"

While signing movies, posters, and Fleshlights, I kept a constant side-eye watch on the staircase. A few guys went down and came back up. It thrilled me to know their secret.

A couple of hours went by and it was time to take a lunch break.

"So what kind of people use them? Like, mostly?" I didn't have to specify what I was asking about. Mike knew.

"Gay guys. It's always gay guys. I've never seen a girl go down there."

"Is it always blowjobs?"

"Pretty much."

It always struck me as strange that people are quicker to give a blowjob, rather than just have sex. A blowjob is much more intimate . . . it's having someone's genitals in your face.

Your face! Not to mention, sex is something both parties enjoy. Giving a blowjob is hardly stimulating unless there's a reward after. How much I love a guy is in direct correlation with how often I unsolicitedly blow him to completion.

"So do these guys get paid, or it's a free-for-all?"

"No, they just do it for fun. It's usually old guys."

I took a second to imagine two grandpa-looking men taking turns blowing each other through a gloryhole, as a gay porno played above each of their heads, in their respective booths. Did they play the same movie? Did they even watch the movie? Remembering I had run my index finger along the inside of one of the holes, I realized that indirectly, I had touched an old man's dick.

"Oh! I'll show you how we make them." Mike excitedly stood up. He walked over to a shelf and rummaged through some tools. I sat up in my chair, eager. What he took out was a drill attachment, in the shape of a perfect circle the exact size of the holes. "It's my job to drill them," he boasted.

I was impressed. "This is amazing." I took it in my hands and turned it over and over like he had brought me an ancient artifact from Egypt. "Can I take a picture?"

As we walked back to the front of the store where people were lined up to see me, I posted the picture of the gloryhole drill on every social network I had. I texted it to friends with the caption "Guess what this is for." I showed a few of the fans but quickly sensed their interest was forced.

When the signing ended, I looked at my phone. No one had correctly guessed what the magical tool was used for. I individually replied, it's to make gloryholes! Everyone at least pretended to be impressed, except for Roy.

"Are you sure it's not just a hole saw?"

"Wtf is a hole saw," I quickly replied.

"To make doorknobs."

Aha.

This tool did not solely exist for the purpose of making holes for old men to suck other old men's dicks through. It was used by normal people, for normal household things. Not letting this newfound discovery bring me down, I continued to spread the instructions of how to make a gloryhole. At the airport, despite my strange run-in the day before, I showed a fan who came to take a picture with me.

"Absolutely I'll take a photo with you. Funny thing, I'm actually coming from a store signing, and look what I found . . ."

I sat in my window seat on my flight back to L.A., and closing my eyes, I thought about the last time I had felt like this.

It was at my aunt's house. I was ten years old, playing hide-and-seek with my cousins, and I went into her bedroom, which she shared with my uncle. Snooping around while I hid, I came across the condoms in her dresser. I knew what they were but had no idea how they worked. I took one, put it in my pocket, and brought it to school the next day.

At recess, we blew it up like a balloon. Everyone huddled in a circle on the playground and examined the condom before opening it. We passed it around like a grenade, making sure to handle it with great care, as if dropping it would cause a huge explosion and we'd be left to explain ourselves. When we finally opened it, none of us could be sure if the oiliness left on our hands after touching the condom was supposed to be there or not. We didn't talk about the details of how it went on, or what exactly it was needed for. Probably none of us knew. All we did know is that it was used for sex, and that made it awesome.

The next time I was at my aunt's, I took the first chance I got to run up to her bedroom, and stole another one. This one I would keep for myself. When I went home later that day, I put the condom away under my pillow, and waited for nighttime to come. Dinner lasted forever that evening. All I could think about was that condom, waiting for me under my pillow, waiting for me to come masturbate. When my mother asked me if I wanted to watch a movie that night, I lied. "Mou neru wa," I explained in Japanese. "I'm just going to sleep."

As soon as I got to my room, I checked to see if the condom was still there. It was. I got under the covers, and while holding on to the condom tightly against my chest, I touched myself. How to use it, what it was for, the technicalities were unknown; but it was the closest I had ever been to sex, and that was enough. I stayed up all night masturbating.

When I landed in L.A., I asked Toni if he had gotten my text.

"Oh, that picture? What was it, for gloryholes?" Like everyone else, he was unenthusiastic.

"Exactly! How did you know?"

His only answer was "'Cause you're a weirdo."

When we arrived home, I called Spiegler first thing.

"How was the rest of the trip? You get molested again?" he joked.

"No. But have you ever seen a real-life gloryhole??"

"Actually, no. But why don't you tell me about it."

I was grinning ear to ear. "Well, first of all, guess how they make them . . ."

12
Rule of Twos

My life has a habit of things happening in twos. Before the Thanksgiving molestation incident, I had already been through a similar experience. It was on the train in Japan. I was about eleven years old and was riding alone. The train was crowded, and we were literally packed up against each other, which isn't anything out of the ordinary for rush hour in Tokyo. I stood face-to-face with a man who, at the time, seemed huge, and towered over me. He grabbed my vagina and looked me right in the eyes. I got off at the next stop and waited for the next train to come. It didn't seem like a big deal.

In Japan, sex offenders on the train are so common, they have their own name. Students learn in school that if they get molested, the proper protocol is to point at the man and call him a *Chikan* to bring awareness to the situation. Signs that translate to "Beware of Chikans!" can be seen all over train stations in Japan, complete with a cartoon image of a girl slapping away a man's hand. Japan is strange like that. The most common crimes are molesting in the train, panty-snatching (the Japanese line-dry their laundry in their backyards), and taking upskirt shots of unknowing girls on escalators. Yet, on the news, you hardly ever hear of other crimes. A drive-by shooting is a completely foreign concept. It's considered rude to blow your nose into a tissue in public, but men regularly read pornographic comics on the train.

The first time it occurred to me that things always happen to me twice was during a routine visit with my favorite psychic of the time. Carrie wore all black, including the dye in her long hair. Pale skin, rings on every finger, if you saw her on the street, you'd peg her as a psychic; at the very least, a practicing Wiccan. Initially, this turned me off from her; she seemed too gimmicky, like an actor playing the part of what she actually was. Despite all this, she told me a bunch of things that ended up coming true. So I saw her for a year and change, about once a month. Every time I told her about a new guy I was dating, her first question was "What sign is he?"

Upon telling her, she'd either 1) show approval by smiling and picking up her tarot cards, or 2) roll her eyes and sigh, "Don't even bother."

Visiting these fortunetellers was a habit I had started up young. When I was growing up, my mom would often take me to see psychics, mediums, palm readers, reflexologists, Chinese medicine doctors with translators who could tell what was wrong with my body from one long, extensive look at my tongue. Not that we took it so seriously. It was just something we liked to do together, for fun, whenever we were bored. Our favorite was a woman in Queens, who gave readings in the back of an Indian restaurant in Jackson Heights. We'd eat from the all-you-can-eat curry buffet and take turns getting up from the table to get our fortunes read in the dimly lit reserved table in the corner.

Afterward, both of us swearing no more trips up to the buffet, we'd order the little cheeseballs-in-syrup dish as dessert and share what our futures held in store for us.

"She says I'm going to write a book," I'd excitedly tell her. "I'm going to be hugely successful, and my life is going to be wonderful."

My mom would tell me about how amazing her life was going to be, and we'd take the subway back home to Brooklyn smiling with full stomachs and bright futures.

Years later, when I did get a book deal, I told my friend Dave that I had been told this would eventually be my destiny.

"No offense, but every single person I know has had a psychic tell them they'd write a book," he dryly declared.

As much as I wanted to, I couldn't argue with him.

Upon reading my astrology chart, Carrie informed me the reason the number 2 was so significant in my life was that my Moon is in Gemini—same as Barack Obama, who is biracial, currently serving his second term as president, and had to be inaugurated twice in his first term. I looked back to see things I had done twice. I got chickenpox twice. I'd had two abortions. My first anal scene had to be shot twice, due to camera problems. Even hooking was something I had tried twice. She was right. Many of my major life events had happened in twos.

Except for losing my virginity, I thought. I had done that three times.

The first time was with Jack. He was a year older than me, and went to school with my cousin. We chatted on IM every day after school and had met up a few times. We never went further than third base. (Fingering.)

Are you a virgin? Jack typed one night.

Yah. U?

Oh good, I was scared you weren't. I am too.

But I want to try . . .

Me too.

It was as simple as that. During the summer vacation between eighth and ninth grade, we met up at Jack's house on
Manhattan's Upper West Side while his parents were at work.
After a long walk in Central Park with a joint he had rolled
for the occasion, we went to his bedroom. His brother had
gotten us condoms, and after somewhat of a struggle, he put
one on. It was impressive for a first time; Jack lasted about
ten minutes before he came into the condom. I didn't bleed,
but I was in pain. It was a success.

A month went by with no sex, and Jack and I didn't speak
much after that. I was glad to have gotten rid of my virginity, but at the same time, I didn't want people to know,
either. Already I had people hating on me for giving Dan
Siegel a blowjob in eighth grade. Eventually, I would come
to embrace my reputation as a slut. This was before I was
able to do so.

The first week of highschool rolled around, and Josh Bern-
stein's parents were out of town. I had been hooking up on
and off with Dan since the seventh grade, and as far as he
knew, a blowjob was as far as either of us had ever gone.

"Dan wants to see you in the bathroom," Greg said. He had
been looking all over the party for me. I smiled and followed
him to the restroom in the master bedroom.

When I saw Dan, we went straight into kissing. We must
have made out for over an hour before anything serious started

to happen. Back then, the length of a hookup wasn't determined by when the orgasm came. We'd dry-hump until our
jeans had rubbed us raw, or someone's parents came home;
whichever happened first.

Dan took his dick out and I put it in my mouth. His was
the first penis I had ever seen close-up. The first time I saw
it, about a year prior, I thought he was playing a prank on
me. *That's what a penis looks like?* Before Internet porn had
taken over every computer screen in every country outside
Antarctica, health class was the only place a kid could really
see a penis. It looked so different in the drawings. It looked
fake to me; it seemed too rubbery.

A year later, being more used to having this object in my
mouth, it didn't seem so foreign. After sucking it for a while,
we ended up dry-humping again on the floor, only this time
neither of us had any pants or underwear on. The floor was
cold on my back, but I was too horny to care. Slowly, I felt
the head of his penis get closer to my vagina. First it rubbed
my clit, then lower, closer to where he could enter. Gradually,
more and more of the head was inside me. It was a struggle,
and pain-wise, it was no different from the first time. Dan
was significantly larger than Jack, and he had to push hard
to get even half of it in. It had just started to feel somewhat
okay when he pulled it out and looked at me in horror.

"Did we just have sex?" He got pale.

"I think so." I knew so, but I didn't want to seem like I was
the only one fully aware of what was going on. Dan couldn't
find out how experienced I was.

"This is bad." Dan's brain was visibly racing. "What if you
get pregnant? We didn't even use a condom."

Dan hadn't cum, but in health class we learned that even precum could get someone pregnant. "What should we do?" I acted concerned. Again, I didn't want to reveal how insignificant this was for me.

"I'm gonna go get Greg." Dan dressed and ran out of the bathroom. I was still getting dressed when they opened the door.

"Here's what we're gonna do. You're both coming to sleep over at my house tonight, and my sister is going to buy us a pregnancy test." Greg was taking charge.

Trying to match Dan's anxiety, and lacking any other sort of plan for the night anyway, I did as he said, and spent the night at Greg's house on Roosevelt Island.

"I can't believe I lost my virginity tonight," I kept repeating.

The test, to Dan's relief and my faked surprise, was negative. The next morning I went home feeling proud that I had sex again, and with a hunch that now I could really start *living*. Not only did I have casual sex, but I had slept over at a guy's house and took an (ultimately unnecessary) pregnancy test. I was becoming a woman.

The third time I had sex was a few months later, that New Year's Eve. I went to a party at a pool hall in Brooklyn held by a bunch of kids from a prep school. I met a senior named Walt, and at the end of the night we went back to his place.

As we made out in his bed, and he reached for the condoms in the drawer, I whispered, "I'm a virgin."

This was completely unnecessary. Walt didn't give a shit if this was my first time, or my hundredth. We didn't even attend schools in the same borough. This was the only time we would ever see each other, and we both knew it.

Yet somehow, the idea of giving this random, older boy my virginity was something I couldn't resist faking.

"Are you sure you want to do this?"

I nodded. The fantasy was playing out perfectly.

Walt was gentle and careful not to hurt me. He kept asking, "Are you okay? Does it hurt?"

It turned me on.

We had sex four times that night, and it was the first time I can truly say I *fucked*. We did it in every position, and when he came, he never did it in the condom; rather, he'd take it off and cum somewhere more erotic, like my breasts or face. I didn't have an orgasm, but it was the first time sex felt *good*, in addition to the pain. That night I vowed never to fuck a virgin again.

A few years ago, I was talking with a girlfriend when we realized we both knew Walt. I told her my story, about how I had told him I was a virgin when I really wasn't.

"Oh, he knew you weren't a virgin. He knows Jack. He thought it was really weird you said that."

So I guess that second time didn't count. I had only lost my virginity twice. My psychic was right; everything important did happen in twos.

Haiku

Enema shop-ping.

Walk up to the register.

—Cashier's a hot guy.

13
Giving Thanks

Thanksgiving at Mark Spiegler's is everything you'd imagine it to be. Unorganized, vulgar, and everyone referring to each other as "whores" and "sluts." The entire meal is store-bought, of course, since none of the twelve girls there cook.

I imagine when the rest of the world envisions a "porno agent," a picture of someone identical to Spiegler comes to mind. By no means conventionally handsome, Spiegler is short, fat, and balding. He walks with a limp since his back surgery ten years ago. With his raspy voice and a heavy Jewish accent, people often mistake him as a New Yorker, rather than the Los Angeles native that he is. He never buys his own clothes, but the girls he has represented over the past twenty years have supplied him with an endless stock of black T-shirts with crude sayings written across the chest; "Fuck you you fucking fuck." "Sluts always welcome." "Whoever said money can't buy happiness forgot about prostitutes." That kind of thing.

He is my favorite man in the world.

"Are you wearing socks today? Is your shirt collared?" I called Spiegler before I headed over for the festivities. I'm pretty sure I call him more than any other girl he represents. At least three times a day, I call him to either gossip, whine, or get advice. If for none of those reasons, I'll call just to hear his voice. If something were to happen to Spiegler, I'd just give up right then and there and hold my breath until I died. I would never say it out loud, but he's my best friend.

"You shittin' me? I'm wearing a shirt that says 'Ride the Bangbus.' I'm not wearin' socks, this ain't that fancy."

I can always count on Spiegler's outfit to tell me what the dress code will be. He owns one pair of socks, and he only wears them once a year, to the AVN Awards show. This past year, he attended his cousin's funeral, so he had the opportunity to wear them twice. If Spiegler wears a collared shirt, it means I should probably wear a dress, or at least jeans with a nice top. A T-shirt and no socks, I can wear whatever I want.

I decided on wearing gray leggings with a white baseball shirt to my first Thanksgiving with my pimp. I use the term endearingly; he's not technically my pimp. He only takes 10 percent of my earnings, instead of all of it. Even then, when I go to pay him at the end of each month, he always shaves a few hundred dollars off the total. Spiegler's not in this for the money; he was already a self-made millionaire at the age of twenty. Representing us is more of a hobby, one that he takes very seriously and, oh, by the way, it happens to make him a ton of cash.

Spiegler's house resembles what a hoarder's home might look like if they had a housekeeper. Seemingly useless trinkets, papers, and boxes of unknown contents everywhere, but everything conveniently seems to have its place. I once asked him if there was any order to the mountain of loose papers on the floor of his bedroom.

"Yah," he answered. "The old ones are at the bottom, the new ones are at the top."

It's hard to talk about the Spiegler Girls without sounding like a cult. There's twenty-five of us in total, and we are the most hardcore girls in the industry. Ask anyone. Most porn agencies represent 100–150 girls each, but not Spiegler. He never exceeds his limit of twenty-five, and there's always a waiting list. Often referred to as the "Ari Emanuel of Porn," he only takes the cream of the crop. We aren't the blond girls with all-fake-everything who don't kiss on the mouth. You need a girl who does *everything*, and does it well, you call Spiegler.

Toni and I arrived just in time to overhear Spiegler yelling something about "Miscarriage Soup" in the living room.

"Are you guys talking about Vicky again?" I guessed as I walked in.

"Yah, Donna didn't know she had another abortion," Spiegler said, laughing from across the room. There is no limit to what is appropriate for conversation with him. Once information is sent out into the universe, anything is fair game.

I eagerly joined. "You'd think the girl would learn to stop letting dudes nut in her!"

Toni shook his head. The long afternoon of shit talking had begun. At home, Toni was the boss. But here, with the rest of the Spiegler Girls, this was my world.

Once we sat down to eat, the conversation didn't get any more holiday-friendly.

"Is the stuffing vegan?" Pamela asked.

"Only if being in a turkey's vagina for three hours is considered vegan," Kelly smiled.

"Try this creamed corn," Courtney said as she passed me a paper plate.

"Ahhh, I never get to eat corn." It was true. Corn doesn't digest in an aesthetically pleasing way. "Good thing none of us are shooting anal tomorrow," I joked.

"Jasmine is!" Four girls chimed in unison, and everyone pointed at Jasmine and laughed.

Jasmine had just started shooting anal scenes two months ago. For a Spiegler Girl, she had waited an awfully long time. Starting anal is a very specific tactic in porn. It's a weapon, and you need to pull it out at the exact right moment. You don't want to start off doing anal right out the gate; being new, if you're a good performer, everyone's going to take notice of you anyway. You don't want to wait too long, either, though—once you are off the "hot list," you're off of it for good. It won't matter if you start getting fucked in the ass by elephants; no one is going to care.

The magic moment is when you are at the height of your career. You've probably been in the industry about a year or two, and the buzz around you is going strong. You were nominated for Best New Starlet last year for all the awards shows. All the big companies have already shot you a few times, but no one is sick of you yet.

That's when you play the anal card.

You're already at the top, and starting anal scenes will extend your time there. After a year or so of that, you start DP (double penetration). And then gangbangs.

I swear, I could be a manager. I owe it all to Spiegler. He taught me everything I know about business.

In previous years, I had always gone home to New York City to spend the holiday with my parents, but this year I had a shoot the day before, and it wouldn't have been worth it to fly back for just one day. My parents and I are close, but they, being traditionally Japanese, couldn't care less about the actual meaning of Thanksgiving. It's not fair to label them typical Japanese parents, though; relatively liberal, my father is a photographer, and my mom used to run a not-for-profit organization. They would rather me do something else with my life, something they could brag to their friends about, but in the end, they are happy I'm happy, and they accept what I choose to do for a living. Not going home for the holiday wasn't a big deal.

Plus, I had that weird incident last year. Perhaps subconsciously, I was holding a grudge against Thanksgiving itself.

Spiegler loves telling my Thanksgiving molestation story, and this day was no exception.

"She's talking about rape this and rape that all the time, and when it finally happens, she drops the ball!" No topic was off-limits when it came to a Spiegler joke.

"She like-a-da rape," Jess added.

It's a running joke that I have a rape fantasy. Don't get me wrong, I love rough sex. I love a guy who can dominate me, make me push my comfort zones, and give me a light beating as I orgasm. But rape? No. I don't even like sitting next to strangers on the subway.

"I don't *have* a rape fantasy! It's not a fucking rape fantasy if the rapist is a hot dude who cuddles with me after! You have so much to learn, Baby Jessie." I threw a piece of cornbread at her as she laughed.

At nineteen, Jessie was the youngest of all of us, hence the nickname. I try not to think too much about the fact that I sometimes get paid to have sex with girls born in the nineties. It never really occurs to me as strange, until she questions my casual *My Girl* reference, and in response to my obvious answer, "You know, the Macaulay Culkin movie," she looks even more puzzled.

On the other side of the spectrum, at thirty-four, Dana was the oldest of us. She's also been with Spiegler the longest. I like to think she is the head of our sorority, and she is in an eternal state of hazing everyone around her. After a certain amount of time in porn, you earn the right to be a self-righteous, egotistical bitch. By default, there's an ironic humor to it; we are shunned by pretty much every group of society. Without the self-deprecating-yet-condescending attitude, you'll never make it. We're a lot like she-males in that way.

We had finished our turkey and somehow went from a debate about rape fantasies to Spiegler retelling the story of how he trained his cat to flush the toilet, when Chris decided to announce he invited his girlfriend over. Chris is a photographer, who's been in the business even longer than Spiegler. Living in the same building as each other, it only made sense he would stop by our orphans' feast.

"Who's your girlfriend?" Dana demanded.

"You guys are gonna love her. She's bringing a few of her stripper friends over." Chris took out his phone to find a picture of this supposed girlfriend.

"*Strippers?*" Laila exclaimed. "Ew."

"Why is she bringing *strippers*?" I asked.

"She's a dancer. So are her friends." Chris was getting annoyed at our obvious judgment. "Watch this, she's always goofin' around her house." He started to show us a video on his phone.

"Strippers are gross," Veronica stated, ignoring the video with the rest of us.

"What, are they all gonna come dance for us?" Laila sneered, stink-face in full effect.

"Yah. Just like you're all gonna gape your fuckin' assholes. For them." No one could get us off our high horses quite like Spiegler. I'd call him a pessimist, but he'd probably just turn around and tell me he's a realist.

We couldn't stop laughing. We were talking about strippers like they were Nazis or serial killers. They took their clothes off for a living. From the point of view of pretty much anyone on earth, we ourselves did much, much worse.

"I just hope they're not intimidated by me," Dana sighed.

Spiegler smiled as he watched us laugh. "Who wants pie? Let's eat it before the *strippers* get here."

Haiku

Rub-bing on my clit

Right when I'm about to cum;

Huge cramp in my leg.

14
Craigslist

It was seven years since we dated. At four years, he was my longest relationship.

"Kevin's DEAD!" Dee screamed into the phone. A few years after we had broken up, the two of them had started dating. Dee was my best friend since we were thirteen, and honestly, the two of them were more compatible than Kevin and I had been.

"What?"

"He's fucking dead!" Dee hysterically screamed again, and hung up. I was in my towel, my hair dripping water all over the floor of my apartment in L.A. Rushing as usual, I was scheduled to shoot an anal scene with Mandingo that day. I called her back but her phone went to voice mail. I dialed Jules's number, one of the few numbers I knew by memory from back before cellphones.

"Is it true?"

I immediately knew it was when I heard Jules crying. In the eleven years I had known him, I had never heard him cry.

"Yo, Asa," was all he could get out.

I sat down on my sofa. Everything felt far away, like I was in an underwater bubble and the rest of the ocean was spinning around me in fast-forward. It couldn't be true. Kevin was the one who was supposed to make it, out of all of us. He was the only one who had actually given any consideration to his future, attending business school instead of going to art school or a party school in Miami, or even skipping college altogether, like the rest of us. When everyone else was fighting, Kevin was the one who kept us together. He was the heart of the group.

"They found him in a hotel room this morning. He OD'd." Jules was the closest to him. They had known each other years before Kevin and I had started dating.

"On what?" As I said the words, I realized I didn't want to hear it. "I'll call you back," I said as I was already hanging up.

It's weird what the mind does when you're in shock. Mine took me back to a sunny afternoon in highschool.

"I have an idea. Just go to the living room until I call you back in." Kevin and I had played hooky from school as usual. We were lucky this particular day, as no one was home; meaning we didn't have to find somewhere outside to waste time until 3 p.m., the time we were supposed to get out of school.

I left the room and waited. Kevin's apartment was weird. I didn't know the term back then, but I now realize his dad was a hoarder. He had old shit covering the entire place. I'd call them antiques, but I doubt they were the kind of old things that held any value. Old clocks, toys, and random mechanical parts hung on every square inch of the wall. Even the ceiling fan was old. Walking from point A to point B in a straight line was an impossibility; every foot or so you'd have to turn your body sideways to squeeze in between two or more random items, be it an ancient pinball machine, or an inconveniently placed overflowing bookshelf. The only room in the apartment looking relatively normal was Kevin's room.

"Come in!" Kevin yelled.

I walked back into his room and found him standing, facing the door, the sheet of his bed draped on him, covering him head to toe like a ghost. It was a blue sheet, patterned with tons of little cowboys riding horses.

"What are you doing?" I giggled.

"Don't you notice anything?" Kevin muffled from under the sheet, laughing.

I looked down and realized he had cut a slit in the fabric, and his dick was hanging out, hard. I hadn't noticed, because of the busy pattern. Shaking with laughter, I walked toward him.

"Blow me."

"What?"

"You heard me. I want you to blow me."

I couldn't tell if he was joking or not. "Are you fucking serious?"

"Yah."

So I got on all fours on the bed and blew.

The next day, when we snuck out of school again to go to his apartment, we sat on his bed to realize his stepmom had sewn the hole shut.

I was Kevin's first girlfriend. I took his virginity, but his friends didn't know that. He was about the tenth guy I had slept with, but it was with him that I really explored my sexuality for the first time. As teenagers in New York City, we had to be creative; most New York apartments are small and not ideal for sex while parents are home. We'd go to the stairwell, the roof, even the elevator to fuck. We'd skip school and take the train for an hour and a half to his dad's country house upstate just so we could smoke weed and fuck all day. I wasn't allowed to sleep over at his apartment, but a few nights a week he'd sneak me in after everyone was asleep. We'd have silent sex, and I'd pee in Gatorade bottles throughout the night.

A year before his death, Dee called me in a panic. "Remember Rosie?"

Of course I remembered Rosie. Kevin hung out with her a few times when we had taken a monthlong break from our relationship in my senior year. He swore up and down all they did was kiss, once at the pizza place.

"She *blew* him. He just told me not to tell you but how can I not?"

It had been almost ten years since we were together.

"What? Are you fucking joking right now? Tell me everything."

"He went out to get Phillies so I have to be quick. Remember he told us about the pizza place, how they kissed? Well, apparently they came back here and she fucking blew him! Asa, I'm so mad at him I can't even look at his face. But he made me promise not to tell you."

"That motherfucker! And that stupid bitch! I'm gonna scream!"

"That's what I said! But you can't tell him you know or he'll kill me."

"I'm not gonna say anything. I don't even care. I think. I don't know. That stupid cunt. Just be mean to him today for me."

"Um, duh. He's going to be paying for this for a long time."

I always thought a day would come where I could confront him about Rosie. And we'd have a laugh about it.

I didn't go to the funeral. I bought a ticket to fly into the city, but the morning of the flight I stayed in bed. A part of me felt he wouldn't want me there. We hadn't gotten along for the past few years. He had started dating Dee two years prior, so we'd see each other often, but only communicated when necessary. He resented me for doing porn. He resented me even before that, when I was stripping.

"I've never hated anyone as much as I hate you," he told me in one of the last phone conversations we had.

I lay in bed, watching the time pass by as I missed the flight, and reminisced about one winter evening in my junior year of highschool. My part-time job at the children's bookstore was okay, but I needed more cash to buy things like weed and purses. At least, that's what I told Kevin. He saw right through me.

"How do you not have enough money? Your parents give you an allowance and I pay for everything anyway."

"I don't *want* you to pay for everything! And my allowance is fucking twenty dollars a day; that's barely enough to *eat!* How can you not get it??" I turned around in the swivel chair and pouted. Pushing against his desk with my hand, I started to spin around and around in circles. I would get my way.

For as long as I can remember, I always felt like I didn't have enough money. Throughout my childhood, my parents had been rich and poor many times. They always sent me to an elite private school, but I was never as rich as the other kids in school. There were years we lived in expensive doorman buildings in SoHo and West Village, but there were also years we lived above a bodega in Brooklyn off a stop on the G train.

At nineteen, during the height of my family's brokeness, I married a sports bookie who offered me five thousand dollars a month as an allowance, just for spending; my food, mortgage, and expenses would already be covered. I felt mortified that someone could think I could enjoy life on that little. In the end I got a ten-thousand-dollar allowance.

My views on money have always been confused.

"Asa, that job sounds shady as fuck. I'm sorry I don't want my girlfriend giving random motherfuckers handjobs!"

I had been strolling Craigslist for days. That's what "looking for a job" meant to me; sitting at my boyfriend's computer in my pajamas at 7 p.m., smoking a blunt, watching *The Simpsons*, and periodically hitting the "refresh" button on Craigslist.

The ad read:

Massage therapist needed. No experience necessary, will train. Make your own schedule! Make up to 600 dollars a day call two one two five five five nine two seven five.

I knew exactly what this job was about. I convinced myself that I didn't. I played dumb with Kevin. I brought the spinning chair to a halt.

"I would never fucking do that, you know that! Why would you even go there? Just let me check it out. It's a legitimate massage therapy job. Maybe this is what I want to do after I graduate."

Eventually I persuaded Kevin to come with me to the job interview. He was mad, but I knew he'd get over it. This wasn't the first time I demanded to do something he disagreed with.

Just a few months ago, I met a man in the subway who offered me a gig as an "import model." You know, the girls who stand in bikinis next to cars at trade shows. The man knew I was young, but once I told him I had a fake ID, he assured me "that should work just fine." When I got to the initial photo shoot, it was at the man's apartment in the projects. I did two sets of photos, one in a bikini, one in a dress, all while hoping the whole time I wouldn't get raped. After I left, I never picked up the man's calls again.

Once we got to the midtown address given to me over the phone, Kevin waited outside. Although the building was beautiful, it was definitely residential, which didn't support my case of "This is a legitimate massage therapy job." I could see Kevin grilling me down through the glass door of the lobby as I walked into the elevator. I pretended not to notice.

Upstairs, a man in a silky black robe opened the door. He was some kind of dark Asian—Thai, Filipino, something like that. He was probably in his mid-forties. Immediately, I got creeped out.

"Welcome," he said, as he smiled and extended his hand. I took it. It was eerily soft.

"Hi." I looked around, and everything was either gold or mirrored. There was a flute hanging from a random corner in the ceiling, the significance of which I immediately grasped; a few years back, my mother had flown in a woman from Thailand to redecorate our entire house according to the laws of fen shui. We had flutes, tiny mirrors, fish, dragons, strategically hanging all over our walls. It's still embarrassing to explain when I take someone back home: *Oh, the trashcan is awkwardly right smack in the middle of the kitchen because obviously, the way they built this place, any of the corners, or against a wall would be bad luck. And try not to knock over the cups of salt inconveniently placed throughout the house. Don't mind the sheet we put over the mirror in the bedroom when we go to sleep, either, but it's inauspicious to go to bed facing a mirror.*

The man introduced himself as Bill.

"Totally not his name," I thought as I followed him inside. The rest of the apartment was just as mirrored and gold as the entrance. He showed me the office, explaining, "She's not here right now, but Mia takes all the bookings," and the "massage room," which was a bedroom with a massage table and some candles.

"So, how open are you?" he somewhat discreetly asked.

"Pretty open." I smiled.

"When can you start training?" He smiled back.

"Whenever. I go to school during the day, but I can always skip."

"That's okay, most of our clients like to book in the evening. You charge them two hundred fifty dollars. A hundred goes to us, one-fifty to you. How far you want to go is up to you, but they do expect a release, if you know what I mean. Do you want to train tonight?"

"Sure." I thought of Kevin downstairs, but how long could training take, anyway? He could wait. I'd rather beg for forgiveness later than go downstairs now to tell him I was gonna be another hour.

Bill started to untie his robe.

"Wait!" I blurted out. "You mean—with you?" Surely this man wasn't going to make me train on *him*.

"Yes," Bill calmly answered. "I can show you some basic massage techniques you may not know."

Everything became too real in one second. In my mind, I would be "massaging" hot businessmen—not sleazy Filipino guys named "Bill" with soft hands who wore silk robes and lived in gold apartments. I didn't wanna see this guy's penis, much less touch it.

"Actually, my boyfriend is downstairs waiting for me. Maybe I should come back some other time," I backpedaled.

"It won't take long," Bill said, smiling calmly. "You can even tell him to wait up here if you want."

"It's okay, I'd really just rather come back without him." Maybe I meant it, maybe I was lying. I would decide later.

I left the apartment and rode down the elevator as I thought of what to say to Kevin. Did this man even run a business at all? If I had "massaged" him, would that be it? Was he the only "client"?

Kevin was still mad, smoking a cigarette when I approached him.

"Well?" he asked.

"I got the job. It's legit. I'm gonna think about it." I casually said as I walked toward the subway station.

We didn't say a word all the way back to his house. He made me a bacon, egg, and cheese sandwich, my favorite, and he never brought it up again.

In some ways, I think Kevin knew me better than anyone. But maybe that's just the kind of thing you can only say once someone's passed.

14 (and a half)
Dee

"If I were a stripper, my name would be Candy." I had been thinking about it for a while.

"Mine would be Crystal." Dee apparently had been, too. "We're so old . . . you know we are almost sixteen? Next thing you know, we'll be thirty." This was a conversation familiar to both of us.

I would go on to strip one day, but Dee took another route completely: law school. Eventually she'd drop out and move to Brazil, but she did go.

Sitting on our favorite stoop in the Lower East Side of Manhattan, we were passing a blunt back and forth. This is what we did with most of our time—smoke blunts. I loved weed, but I only smoked socially, when I was with my friends. Eventually, after years of being too high to get up to look for the remote control, I realized I actually liked being sober better. In five years, I'd go on to quit smoking altogether. Not Dee. For her, everything was better with weed. She woke up in the morning and smoked a blunt walking to the subway station on her way to school. She smoked blunts in between classes. She smoked blunts after school, and smoked blunts on her evening dog walk before bed. To this day, she doesn't do anything unless it consists of a pregame blunt before, and a celebratory blunt after. Blunt in between preferred.

By definition, we were potheads. But that didn't mean we didn't do other things, too. Acid, Ecstasy, angel dust, my mom's Ambien—thankfully, we never liked coke. We partook in recreational drugs almost every weekend. In particular, we loved Special K—ketamine, K, liqs, animal tranquilizer. We'd buy bottles whenever we could afford to, cook the liquid up into a powder, and scrape it up and into our noses. We loved to snort it lying in my bed together, staring at a certain hole in my bedroom wall—as the high spread throughout our bodies, the hole would get farther and farther away.

Dee is my best friend in the universe. We haven't lived in the same country for over seven years now, but it doesn't affect her place in my life. I knew her before either of us had ever even smoked a cigarette for the first time. We were thirteen, and although we were in different classes, we took after-school music together because we were both failing. We were the only ones in the class. It turned out we got along, and soon we'd skip the class and go eat pizza together after school instead. We liked the same kinds of boys, music, and TV shows. We were both only children. We both moved to the United States a couple of years ago, and we both were middle-class kids on scholarship, living among trust fund babies. We lived close to each other—her in the Lower East Side, me in SoHo—so we'd take the same bus home in the evening.

From that year on, we were inseparable. We were always the two girls in a group of boys. Wherever I went, she went. Whatever boy she was dating, I was dating his best friend. Sometimes we'd switch. When highschool came around, we were sent to different schools, but we remained as close as ever.

"Where do you wanna spend the night?" Dee asked, ashing the blunt on one of the steps. "Devon is getting some acid tonight if we want. We could drop it at his place and walk fifty blocks back to my house if you want."

So it was decided. We would spend the night at Dee's.

Across the street we saw a man wearing our favorite outfit— baseball hat, North Face jacket, and some Air Force Ones on his feet. Dee and I looked at each other.

"He's cute."

"I was thinking the same thing."

"Let's get a closer look."

We put out the blunt, got up off the stoop, and crossed the street. As we got closer and closer, something seemed off about the man—he seemed to be talking to himself. Closer still, and we saw under his North Face jacket was a ratty sweatshirt and jeans. His shoes, which were once a drawing point, were old and filthy. And what was that scent? The nearer we got to him, the more it smelt like piss.

As we passed by him and caught a glimpse of his face, covered in dirt, and a mouth without teeth, we both looked down at the ground as we realized he was a homeless crackhead. Not even a hot one.

We kept walking, ashamed of our poor judgment. Neither of us admitting to the situation, we continued to another stoop in silence.

That night we dropped a tab of acid each in Devon's bed. We watched cartoons and laughed our asses off, before deciding on taking our much-anticipated walk.

Walking back to Dee's house was everything we had hoped for. I felt like I was in a winter wonderland. My legs shook like Jell-O; my eyes played tricks on me. It's kind of frightening, how much a drug can really alter your reality. Although I was aware I was tripping, everything around me was just *different*, in the most pleasant way. The cold didn't bother us; we both glided down the fifty blocks, a little over two miles, with our jackets open.

Getting into her building, the fluorescent lights hit us— and the lighting/temperature/atmosphere adjustment got me feeling weird. We awkwardly stumbled into Dee's apartment, even more awkwardly said hi to her parents, and jetted for her bedroom. Laughing over nothing, Dee pulled out a Baggie from her purse with another tab in it. "Should we split it?"

We should have looked at the clock right then, because then we would have known it was already midnight, far too late to be dropping anything. We also should have known that we were tripping pretty hard already, and taking more would only work against us. The thing about acid is that it's such a huge commitment. You will absolutely not sleep for the next eight hours, and you will definitely, 100 percent, utter the words "When am I gonna stop tripping?" by the end. Sure, it's fun to see the world through a kaleidoscope. *For the first five hours*. Those last three tick by in slow motion.

So we didn't look at the clock, we didn't use our better judgment, and because of our impaired vision, it took us probably another hour to split the tab with a razor Dee found in her makeup drawer. As soon as we dropped it, we started tripping harder. We went from giggling schoolgirls to autistic zombies.

"Why did we do that?" Dee looked at me in horror. As the words came out of her mouth, her face turned into a leopard. The next eight hours would be shitty.

We tried to watch cartoons. It was unavoidable, though—
we were each descending further into our own internal hell.

"Let's just try to go to sleep," I suggested, wanting to be
alone. I knew she felt the same.

We got into our respective beds, both of us in the fetal position, facing away from each other. I closed my eyes tightly so
that I wouldn't have any more visuals. The acid didn't let me
escape so easily—I saw patterns on the insides of my eyelids.

"My room is so fucking dirty," Dee would periodically say
through her tight jaw. "I can't stand it."

I had to pee. But my body was so uncomfortable—my own
skin was so foreign-feeling, I didn't have it in me to get up
to go to the bathroom. My back ached from every muscle in
my body clenching, my skin felt itchy, and my mouth tasted
weird. Besides, what if her parents were still awake? I wasn't
presentable.

Then my underwear started to feel wet.

No. No. This isn't happening. Did I just piss myself?

Too embarrassed to say anything to Dee, I got up to go to
the bathroom. Her parents were asleep already, to my relief,
because halfway to the bathroom I had to get on my knees
to crawl. I opened the bathroom door and climbed onto the
toilet as I pulled my pants down.

What the fuck. Dry.

Not only had I not pissed in the bed, but once I did sit
down, I didn't have to go anymore. I flushed the toilet, to
keep up what I thought was a façade, and crawled back to
the room.

I repeated this eleven more times throughout the night.

A few hours into cradling ourselves to silence, Dee got up to turn the computer on. "I'm playing music," she whispered.

She put on 50 Cent's "Many Men," and I thanked her almost immediately. I had never heard the song before; it was right when 50 Cent was really starting to blow up.

The song ended, and came on again. Dee had put it on repeat. It must have repeated a hundred times that night. The mellow beat, the almost lullaby-like chorus, put me into a trance, where I wasn't convincing myself I had wet the bed every ten minutes. Eventually, it rocked us to sleep.

The next morning we woke up and walked over to Chelsea's house to smoke weed.

"Last night was weird," I told her.

"I think that was the last time I'll ever do acid," Dee added.

I agreed.

"The weirdest fucking part," I added after a few minutes, "was that fucking guy we saw. We saw a bum and thought he was a hot guy!"

Chelsea laughed.

Diary, 2012–2013

January 30

It's a little late but it's a new fucking year. I'm quitting cigarettes tomorrow. Also, no more pizza. I've been ordering two large thin crust pies for myself everyday at 11 a.m. since I got back from Vegas seven days ago (was there for the AVN Awards and convention, so naturally, I was starving the whole time), and it's time to get back to the routine. It's nothing but smoothies and salads from here on out.

I'm also committing to keeping a journal.

The last time I had anything like this was when I was in highschool. In the back of my diary, on the blank sheet between the last lined page and the back cover, I wrote down the names of all the boys I had hooked up with. If I hooked up with them multiple times, they would have a tally next to their name, a scratch for every time we messed around.

David ////
Perry
Josh W //
Zach ///
Tyler /
Etc.

On the lined sheets I wrote about my sexual escapades, starting from my very first French kiss on the school bus in fourth grade, to losing my virginity when I was thirteen, to getting fucked spread eagle by highschool seniors on rooftops alongside my girlfriends. I wrote about trying Ecstasy when I was twelve, but how it had failed to work because we split the one pill we had five ways. I wrote about shoplifting sprees, huffing Dust-Off in the school bathroom, and tagging along with boys on graffiti missions in the middle of the night.

My mom found my diary and read it one weekend when I had told her I was going to stay with Dee. The truth was that I had gone up to New Jersey with a boy to a three-day outdoor rave. I stopped taking her calls, and when she called Dee's mom, she knew I was up to no good. I came home to her sitting at the dining table crying, asking me where she'd gone wrong as a mother.

"Are you using condoms at least?" she sobbed in Japanese.

"Obviously!" I screamed back in English.

I was lying.

That was the day I stopped documenting my life.

Sorry, Mom.

January 31

Already smoked again. But so far so good on the no pizza thing.

February 3

Woke up with pizza crumbs in my bra. I disgust myself. Anorexia starts tomorrow, since there is still some left.

I guess I may as well smoke a cigarette now and start everything fresh tomorrow.

February 5

I've decided it's unhealthy to just stop smoking cold turkey. I'm cutting down to three a day, and then eventually two a day, then one . . .

It's Super Bowl Sunday. I hate football. Almost as much as I hate commercials.

February 6

It's hard to hate on Mondays when it entails having sex for money.

February 7

Shot a scene with Jordan today. He talks too much. He kept saying "I don't *want* to be a big star. I don't *want* to be doing this when I'm fifty years old."

It was kind of a buzzkill. But his dick felt good.

P.S. Three-cigarettes-a-day thing is working out! Think I'll cut down to two soon.

February 9

Holy fuck. I was getting my makeup done at Nichole's today when her roommate Krissy came out of her room to chat.

I'm pretty sure my life has changed.

She was telling me about a cleanse she's been doing. It's basically anorexia; she ingests nothing but water for seven days. During the cleanse, every morning she gives herself a coffee enema.

"It's exactly what it sounds like—an enema using coffee. You just fill the bag with diluted coffee and hold it in for twenty minutes. It's good for detoxifying your liver and kidneys."

She had me at enema.

As I type this, clenching my asshole and holding the coffee inside me, I can feel the effects of the caffeine coursing through my body. I drink coffee every day, can't even speak without my first cup in the morning, but this is different. I can literally feel my energy going up by the minute.

I have an extremely addictive personality. Throughout my life I've been addicted to opiates, coffee, cigarettes, exercise, and possibly sex (still pending). When I find a food I like, it's all I eat for breakfast, lunch, and dinner. I meet a guy I like, and I want to be by his side twenty-four hours a day, seven days a week.

I think I just found my new thing. Gonna google if there are any negative side effects!

February 11

Got woken up at three in the morning by this text from Spiegler:

"This just in! What's something 9 out of 10 people enjoy?

"Gangrape."

February 12

It's officially been a whole year since my last car accident.

What a long way I've come. I should do something crazy to celebrate.

It took me two years to get my driver's license.

I resent all Asians-can't-drive jokes, or even women-can't-drive jokes. In New York City, we don't drive. We just don't. Our public transportation system is so good, it gets us to our destinations in a shorter amount of time than a car would. Additionally, parking is so inconvenient, that even if you are lucky enough to find a spot on the street, you're still likely walking another five to ten blocks to wherever you're ultimately going.

I moved to California at the age of twenty-five. For the first six months I lived here, I didn't drive. Relying on drivers and the occasional taxi (which, by the way, are crazy expensive in L.A.), I was miserable. Growing up in New York, I wasn't used to not being able to leave a place exactly the moment I wanted. I'd finish shooting my scene, and then have to wait another thirty minutes before I could leave to go home.

So I bought a car. I didn't know how to turn it on, and I couldn't drive it off the lot myself, but I purchased a Prius. My friend Van, who I was living with at the time, had to drive it home for me. In this car, I would learn to drive.

"I can't fucking do this. I don't know why I bought this stupid thing," I cried on my first attempt. Van and I had been circling our residential neighborhood at twenty miles an hour. If I could give one piece of advice on learning to drive, it would be this: Don't learn from your friends. You will fight.

I googled "learn to drive in Los Angeles" and found a driving school in my area. When I got in the car, the instructor
looked at me funny.

"So why don't you know how to drive?" he asked. I explained I was from New York, and he nodded like he under-
stood. I asked him if I was his oldest student. He assured me
I wasn't, but his face told me I was.

Eventually, I got a hang of the whole thing. I started to
drive my own car, first just to and from set, and then gradually everywhere. I even drove myself to San Francisco for a
dancing gig, which was an eight-hour drive away. I passed
the written test to get my permit on the first try. I was ready
to become a licensed driver.

Feeling confident, I went online to make an appointment
for the actual driving test. None of the DMVs close by had
anything available for the next month. I started to look at
the DMVs farther away, and found one in Lancaster that had
an opening in two weeks. I took it. "I can't wait that fucking
long to get my license! I'm sick of driving around illegally,
panicking every time I pass a cop car," I argued to Van. An
hour wasn't too long of a drive. We would do it.

The drive there was exciting. After today, I'd be a licensed
driver. I couldn't wait to post it on my Facebook, and show
off to all my New York friends. "Look at me! I'm a driver!" I
planned on posting a picture of myself in my car, possibly
even with the employee who would grant me my license. I
insisted on doing the driving to Lancaster. "It's enough that
you're coming with me," I explained to Van.

As I parked my car upon finishing the test, I felt confident.
No way I didn't ace that, I thought. The testing lady went

through her list, and explained to me all the things I did wrong. *Just get on with it*, I thought. *We both know I passed.* Imagine my surprise when the words "Unfortunately, I can't pass you" came out of her mouth. I was floored. I was so sure I had done a good job.

Outside my window, I saw a teenage girl jumping with excitement out of her car to go hug her parents.

I sheepishly got out of the car and shook my head "no" when I spotted Van waiting for me. He knew what it meant.

The drive back from Lancaster was long. Having completely lost the confidence I had ten minutes ago, I asked Van to drive. I stared out of the window the whole ride home, tears flowing out of my eyes. "I never want to drive again," I swore.

I repeated this same long-ass trip to and from Lancaster two more times over the next few months, before I had to take another written test to get my permit again. The permit is only good for three driving tests; after that, you lost that, too.

Eventually, I gave up on getting my license. I would just drive illegally forever. Surely, not every driver I saw on the freeway was licensed? There had to be people who were too busy to go to the DMV and wait all day. Plus, I was only driving illegally when there wasn't a licensed driver over the age of twenty-one in the passenger's seat. I did everything I could to justify it in my head.

My first ticket came a year after I started driving. It was late at night, and I was heading home from set. Still in my full-on porno hair and makeup, I was texting while driving on the empty freeway. When I got pulled over, the cops flashed their flashlights in my eyes. "We thought you were drunk driving," one of them told me. Not that it was a surprise, but I was offended. My driving skills were so poor, they thought I was drunk. They saw I clearly wasn't drunk and didn't bother to ask for my license. I got off easy this time.

Over the next year, I would get pulled over once every month or so; I forgot to turn on my headlights, I was texting, I didn't stop at the sign, that sort of thing. I quickly learned that having my videos in the car would come in useful. I only got one ticket, which was for "driving without a license."

That cop was probably gay.

February 13

Guess who's back—Toni Ribas!! He has me booked for his production tomorrow, and of course I'll be doing my scene with him!

So excited . . . I haven't seen him in months!! He's a Spanish director/performer so I only get to see him a few times a year . . .

I hope he takes me out after . . .

February 14

My scene with Toni was fucking amazing. As usual. How romantic, right? An anal scene with my favorite cock on Valentine's Day.

Shooting a scene always makes me feel a little bit in love, but with Toni it's different . . . I still want to hang out with him after the sex. I want to sleep in bed with him and wake up with him in the morning.

I asked him to take me to the movies tomorrow, and he said he would. Agghhh!!

February 16

Toni took me to the movies last night and then slept over. I've missed him fucking me . . . I hope he comes back tonight.

February 23

I've been hanging out with Toni every single day. It sucks 'cause I know he's gonna go back to Spain soon . . .

I shot with a girl today who stuck her finger in my belly button while we post-scene showered. I freaked out. You can stick your entire hand inside my asshole, but don't you dare put even the tip of your finger in my belly button.

I'm cringing just thinking about it.

February 26

Real whores work on Sunday.

Off to my shoot.

February 27

Went to get massages with Toni today. I blew him before the massage, when the masseuses left the room so we could strip down and get under the sheets. He told me, "Fuck happy endings; if I had a place, they would give happy beginnings."

I think he's on to something?

March 2

Guess what.

1. I had pussy every day this week.
2. Toni extended his stay in L.A.! He thought he was going to have to go to Greece for a production, but it's delayed! Yayy!!

March 6

I just learned what a "Power Bottom" is. It's someone who is enthusiastically submissive. I think that's me.

March 8

Been dancing in Hawaii for the past two nights. I miss Toni : (
Sunbathing by the pool before I get ready for my last night in my blue thong bikini.
The lady next to me is not amused.
But her husband is.

March 11

Heading to Cabo for vacation with Toni!
There is a serious abundance of white boys with mustaches on this flight.

March 14

Cabo is fucking magical. I'm starting to really fall for Toni. He's in the shower now . . . I feel like I am falling in love.

I met Toni three years ago. It was before I had ever done an anal scene, before I had hardly even had much anal sex in general. Being a fan of his, I requested him for a boy-boy-girl threeway scene, and I was so turned on by him, it turned into my first anal scene, and ended as my first double penetration scene.

The next day, I called him and went over to his apartment. He was still living in Spain at the time, so he had rented a small one-bedroom apartment in the Valley whenever he was in the United States—which was only a few months out of the year. He came down to get me in the parking lot, and we fucked as soon as we got up to his apartment.

I was in his bathroom, sitting on the toilet waiting for the cum to fall out of my pussy, when I noticed red flag number one. A bottle of conditioner.

A bottle of conditioner in a single man's bathroom is much more than just a hair maintenance product. It is a symbol of another woman's presence. Not just a woman, but most likely women. This man likely fucks either 1) so many women that he was sick of hearing "Why don't you have conditioner??" or 2) one woman so often that she brought her own bottle of conditioner to keep at his house. No man buys a bottle of conditioner for himself, unless he has long hair—which is a red flag in itself, and in which case, I wouldn't be sitting on his toilet with his cum slowly dripping out of my pussy in the first place.

I have a few rules when it comes to dating, some things that I absolutely do not look over or let go. I'll meet the perfect man, but if he is guilty of defying one of these rules, I walk away as soon as I can.

"I gotta go, I have to go meet Spiegler." This was my go-to excuse to leave at the time. Now it's "I gotta go, I have to clean my ass for tomorrow's anal scene." It's usually true.

We fucked one more time, and I left. Over the next month, I continued fucking him, but I never treated it seriously. He fucked me in a way that had me entranced, and it was the best sex I had ever had in my life—which was saying a lot.

Toni has one of the strongest Spanish accents I've ever heard. Because of this, whenever he called, I hit "ignore" and texted him, making up an excuse as to why I couldn't physically talk on the phone. In person was one thing—I could see his facial expressions, hand gestures, etc. and we communicated just fine. But on the phone, without any visual help, I could barely understand a third of what he said. For this, we texted a lot. And here is where red flag number two lay.

The emoticons.

I see you tonight :)

Can't wait to fuck you >.<

Come over : p

A man who is so well versed in emoticons can only mean one thing: He texts many, many women.

But on the bright side: He has no kids, isn't "best friends" with any of his exes, isn't a registered sex offender (I asked), and he doesn't wear Crocs. I think I'm willing to overlook a couple of red flags.

March 15

Back home from Cabo.

We are both sick as fuck. We both have a cold and Toni has pinkeye in both eyes.

It's eighty degrees outside but we have the fireplace going.

Maybe going in the Jacuzzi in Mexico wasn't such a good idea after all.

March 20

I'm in Florida, and I'm still sick as fuck. I'm supposed to be shooting but I swear I'm too sick.

Last night when I landed, I told Spiegler I wouldn't be able to shoot today. He texted the producer for me:

"Asa just landed in Miami, but she isn't feeling well.

"She has a fever.

"She isn't a complainer, so please go easy on her tomorrow if she isn't 100%."

Not a complainer. Ha-ha-ha.

March 21

Feeling a little better. Rocked my anal scene. Going back to bed.

March 23

Currently on the plane to Vegas for a shoot.

1) It's 2012. There should be moving walkways everywhere. My favorite thing to do is walk at a normal pace on a conveyor belt (is that what they're called?) and see all the people I pass who walked on normal ground.

2) People who travel with their own pillows are probably assholes.

April 1

Shot a DP scene today with Toni and Michael. I feel like this might be the last time Toni and I shoot this kind of scene together . . . His face looked angry while Michael was fucking me.

I liked it.

April 10

Did an interview for a documentary about Hello Kitty. I think they were trying to make me cry. They told me about a pedophile who lured victims in with Hello Kitty, as opposed to the usual candy . . . I stayed strong and didn't let out a single tear.

I'm pretty impressed with myself that I made it out of highschool without a Hello Kitty tattoo. That's exactly the kind of idiot I was (am?).

April 11

Just had the best fucking sex ever. At one point Toni hit my face a little too hard and now my lip is turning blacker by the minute . . . I kind of like it. I keep pressing the bruise with my finger. It hurts kind of good.

I went to get hash from the clinic this morning (for Toni) and I'm pretty sure I got high just by being there. I was scared to change lanes on the freeway, so I drove 50 mph on the far right lane all the way to set.

April 12

The XRCO Award show was tonight. I won three awards, including Performer of the Year!

For the most part I think my black lip was covered by my lipstick.

I still brought it up to every person I ran into, "Hey, how've you been? By the way, this black lip is from sex, not domestic abuse." I think it ultimately made me sound more suspicious.

I also just realized, why don't women whose husbands beat them just say that they are into kinky sex? I mean they always give the old "I fell down the stairs," or "I walked into the door again, I'm so clumsy," which no one believes anyway. Domestic abuse is obviously wrong, but if they're gonna stick through it and give excuses, why not give a believable one?

April 21

I've always wanted to see someone slip on a banana peel.

April 22

I'm down to three cigarettes a day, but I'm stuck—No matter how hard I try, I can't do less than three!

I'm fine when I'm on set; it's when I'm at home . . . I need to get a hobby. The writing is one, but it's not enough. WHAT ELSE IS THERE?

April 23

Bought SingStar for the PlayStation, Toni and I have been karaoke-ing all day with the windows wide open.

I'm really only good at one song, which is "You Know I'm No Good," by Amy Winehouse. I play it over and over and sprinkle in a little Britney here and there.

Bet my neighbors wish I'd go back to smoking on the balcony and fucking loudly.

Also:

They asked me to host the AVN Awards this year!

Holy fuck. What am I going to wear? What if I trip?

I'm so excited.

April 26

Getting really good at SingStar. It's now a daily ritual, wake up at six, drink coffee, sing for half an hour (windows open, of course), work out, go to work.

May 17

Just woke up in San Francisco, dancing here for the next three nights.

I can't stop masturbating, but that's okay—I don't have to be anywhere for another seven hours.

May 19

I fucking love this club! Money is great, and they let me do a dildo show at the end of my set. I'm not a good dancer, so any kind of distraction is a good one.

The only thing I hate is the one-dollar bills. I'm too embarrassed to use them, so I end up leaving thousands of dollars' worth of singles in my car, for "valet money." It's strange, I don't even think twice before I show my inner organs to the world—but paying for things in one-dollar bills is just too mortifying.

May 23

Just saw the review for a scene I did and I can't believe my eyes.

It's for a site called Shesgonnasquirt.com. The funny thing about that, is that I'm not a squirter. It can happen, but I'm not in control of it; if a guy knows how to finger me and press all the right buttons to make me squirt, then it happens. It doesn't necessarily feel good, or bad. I'm still not sure if it's piss, or something else; if it's really supposed to coincide with orgasming, or if it's just a myth, like blue balls, or "just the tip."

"I'm telling you, I'm not in control of it," I fucking told Spiegler when he called me about the booking. "I can't guarantee I'll squirt."

"I told them. They want you anyway."

When I got to set that day, Dave explained to me what was going to happen. They were going to cut during the sex, fill a disposable douche up with water, empty it into my vagina while the penis was in my asshole, and start rolling the camera again when the water was all coming out of me. I had seen scenes like this before and thought they were completely unbelievable and embarrassing for everyone involved. But being that I was already on set, and the male talent was one of my favorites, Johnny, I kept my mouth shut and went along with the plan.

The scene was every bit as ridiculous as I had predicted. About three times per position, we cut and did the douche trick. So much water came out, and there's no way with that many cuts, the scene came out looking smooth. I was so sure everyone was going to know this was fake.

But today. Today I read the reviews.

"I've watched Asa a hundred times, and I've *never* seen her squirt like that!"

It's too much sometimes.

What's the deal with squirting. Is it piss? It doesn't feel like it coming out, but sometimes it has a slight yellowish tint to it, and it certainly smells and tastes like it. Does it coincide with cumming, ever? It didn't for me, but I had seen numerous movies where it seems like the squirting happens while girls have the most intense orgasms of their lives. Were they just exaggerating for the camera, like me? Or am I missing out on something amazing?

May 27

Been shooting nonstop since I got back from SF. Got into an argument on set today on whether or not blue balls are real. I called bullshit; it's just a way for guys to get their nut off.

I got home and asked Toni if they're real. He said no. But I can't tell if he just wanted me to shut up.

June 1

Toni shit with the door open today. I acted disgusted but I'm secretly super-excited. We are a real couple now.

June 7

I just spent the last two hours reading sixty-six pages of ce-
lebrity gossip on the Perezhilton.com. If I didn't have anal
sex on camera for a living, I'd be a total waste of human life.

June 10

Today is the Puerto Rican Day parade in NYC. More like the
Puerto Rican Day Rape parade. I swear someone gets raped
there every year.

No one in L.A. has heard of it.

I remember in highschool my friend Christina's brother
was in jail 'cause he allegedly raped someone at the parade
in 2001. She told me he was innocent.

"They all are," I told her. We both knew what I meant.

June 15

Fucking shit! I didn't get off set until 2 a.m. last night, and
halfway home, I got a flat tire. I was too tired to change my
outfit to go home, so I was wearing a mini T-shirt that said
"Will Flash for Booze" across the chest.

This is exactly how rapes happen!

Luckily Anastasia was still up and came to get me. Her
roommate changed my tire while we sat in her car and sang
Alanis Morrisette songs.

June 18

Just finished the first night of a dance gig in Atlantic City, tanked. And I mean . . . tanked. Archie (my roadie) kept saying, "That was fucking brutal" every time we returned to the greenroom.

There were never more than six guys surrounding the stage. And the stage was huge. In one corner were two black guys who didn't look at me once, no matter how hard I tried to force their attention on me. I walked all the way across the stage, about twenty seconds, to the opposite corner, to a drunk man who stingily fed me single dollar bills. I thought he was a fan, until I leaned in close to him and he asked me what my name was.

Tonight I felt like how the world portrays strippers: sad, pathetic, futureless.

People might say dancing on a stage, peeling off piece by piece a bikini that was already skimpy to begin with, for a crowd of horny guys, is degrading. But what's actually degrading is stripping to a sparse, almost-empty crowd of indifferent men who don't even notice if my nipples are out or not. And don't care.

It was mortifying. My ego took a hit, for sure. I started dancing a year ago, which was already four years into my career—I've never danced to a crowd that wasn't full of eager fans waiting to shower me with money.

Was it the venue? Was it the promoter? Or is it my biggest fear . . . that my name simply didn't draw a crowd?

Selling merch was worse. I sold two DVDs and two lapdances. I'm currently too discouraged to even count my money, but I'm certain I didn't make enough to even cover Archie's fee tonight. It will have to come out of the money paid to me directly from the club—something I've never done. I always pay Archie out of the money I make onstage—I don't even dip into the merch money, let alone my check for the gig itself.

I dance again tomorrow night. If I have a few more gigs like this, my soul will start feeding on itself for emotional nutrition and eventually you will be able to look into my eyes and see that they are empty; void of anything, dead inside. Sad, pathetic, futureless.

June 22

I got home today to find my Fleshlight disassembled and drying out on Toni's bathroom sink. Half of me is flattered; the other half is scared it feels better than me.

July 2

Toni just fucked me prison-style while an Adele song played in the background. If that's not romantic, I don't know what is.

Speaking of which:

Sixty-Nine: Overrated. Prison-style: Underrated.

July 4

Happy Birthday, America. I had sex in you for money today.

July 6

Toni left for Spain today. He'll be back in a month. Wahh.

July 8

I shot a DP scene at 8 a.m. today, got home around noon, and laid on the sofa like a useless piece of shit until the sun went down and I had to get up to turn the lights on.

That's the saddest thing sometimes, that moment where it's bright one second, you're watching TV, browsing the Internet, texting your friends . . . and then all of a sudden it's dark as fuck and you're alone in your living room like a lonely idiot.

I keep thinking I've done nothing productive today, but then I remember, "Oh yah. I did double anal this morning. I'm good," and I go back to watching a rerun of *Teen Mom* that I've already seen at least twice.

July 11

Heading to Toni's home in Spain today for vacation. I don't think I'll have time to write there.

July 12

This plane ride is the most boring thing I've ever done in my life.

Sometimes women shit while giving birth. I just found out. I wonder if anyone has ever shit in their baby's eye by accident while giving birth, and in turn, that baby got pinkeye?

If I ever give birth, I'm gonna clean my ass out with an enema the second I go into labor.

July 14

Toni's house here is gorgeous! I'm swimming in his pool every day. I want to look like a beautiful mermaid so I wear my gold bikini and swim with my eyes closed. Goggles are for nerds.

July 16

I give up on looking beautiful. Not only am I succumbing to goggles; I'm wearing a latex swimming cap that makes me look bald and hides my eyebrows so I look like a cancer patient. My bikini keeps falling off so I just go naked now. I guess this will be a true test of Toni's love.

We shot an anal scene for my website today in front of an abandoned castle. I had to hike up a mountain in my slutty porno clothes, but it was worth it.

July 17

I was texting Mia today, and my phone autocorrected "Asperger's" into "Superheroes." Kind of beautiful.

July 24

Just got to Venice and holy fuck, it's the most beautiful thing I've ever seen in my whole life. Like it's breathtaking. We stopped in St. Tropez, and Toni's beach house in Spain (forgot the name of the town) on the way.

Toni's family was at the beach house, too. We didn't have sex the whole three days we were there. I've never been so horny.

Everything here is really old, and you can't get anywhere without riding a gondola (boat). Our paddler (is that what they're called? boat driver?) sang just like in the movies. I feel magical being here.

July 27

Toni put a plastic bag over my head while he fucked me today.

You can't say I'm not living dangerously.

July 31

Watching the Olympics, we are back in Toni's Barcelona house. Is it just me, or are gymnasts getting fatter? I thought they were supposed to be so anorexic that their periods stopped . . . or was that ballerinas?

September 1

Vacation officially over, back in L.A. Luckily, I didn't find my dignity. I'll be back on set tomorrow.

Currently feeling very international. Americans are cultureless.

September 15

Last night I cried my eyeballs out. It's too embarrassing to even say why.

I got home from my DP scene, and still horny when I got home, I went straight for Toni's dick.

He told me, "I just jerked off before you got here."

So I left him alone.

Later at night when we were watching a movie, I asked him what he thought about when he jerked off. I don't expect him to think about me, but I guess I was just curious. And I guess secretly a part of me was hopeful he would say he thought about me.

This motherfucker proceeds to tell me he went on to a webcam website and jerked off while a girl showed him her ass.

What the fuck?

I laughed it off, continued to watch the movie, but less than five minutes later I was uncontrollably crying. Toni acted annoyed (which I guess is reasonable) and that made everything worse and basically I ended up crying in the guest room all night, screaming, "Why couldn't you just lie to me, whyyyyy?!"

I don't even know why I'm being so sensitive. It's not even realistic to think he would jerk off thinking about the person he has sex with in real life, every single day. But for some reason I am deeply, deeply offended. It just goes to show you—for every woman you jerk off to, there's a tired husband/boyfriend/significant other jerking off to some other bitch.

October 5

Bored makes me horny makes me masturbate makes me useless makes me bored makes me horny makes me masturbate makes me useless makes me bored makes me horny makes me masturbate makes me useless makes me bored . . .

October 19

Fuck. My period is late. I can't even think about this right now. Toni is the only one who cums inside of me but . . . What if??? I can't even think about this right now.

October 20

Period still not here. Freaking out.

October 21

Omg thank fucking god thank you thank you thank you I got my period today. Phew!

I've been pregnant twice before.

The first time was when I was nineteen. I hardly remember it. It was with Eddie, and at the time, it really didn't seem like a big deal. Most of my friends had been through an abortion, and if anything, I was excited to join them in the ranks of women who had had that experience.

The second time was different. I was twenty-one, and the baby belonged to the same guy. I was doing tons of Oxy, so the morning sickness wasn't an issue; I was throwing up every day anyway.

When I found out, I had been doing the master cleanse. It's a detox program, designed to cleanse your liver and kidneys, but I was doing it to lose weight. Basically, it's anorexia with a twist. Food is forbidden; the only thing ingested is a mixture of hot water, lemon juice, maple syrup, and cayenne pepper. I, of course, was ingesting OxyContin in addition.

The cleanse itself is miserable. You can't go out, because you have no energy. You can't hang out with people, because they'll eventually have to eat, and the temptation is too much to resist. You can't even watch TV, because the risk of a food commercial playing, or a character in a show eating, is too high. I don't know how I did it, but I made it to ten days.

On the tenth day, I don't know what prompted me, but I took a pregnancy test. My period was always fucked-up because of 1) the opiates and 2) the fact that I was always forgetting to take my birth control pill. The test came back positive. Fucked-up from having ingested nothing but painkillers and lemon juice for the past ten days, I hardly had the energy to call anyone. Eddie and I were breaking up, and we hadn't even spoken for weeks; I certainly didn't have the energy to deal with him. I called my friend Jay.

"I'm pregnant."

He took me to the same abortion clinic I had been to before. There's nothing quite as humbling as going in for an abortion and your name already being on file. Embarrassingly familiar with the process, we zipped through the building easily. When it came time for my sonogram, I was informed I had been pregnant for three months already.

"Would you like to see the baby?" the doctor asked. I declined her offer.

"Because of how far along you are in your pregnancy, we'll need to put sticks in you today to stretch out your cervix. We can continue with the procedure tomorrow."

I didn't understand what she meant, but I agreed to go ahead with it. I knew I didn't want a baby. Especially not with my ex.

They showed me the "sticks," and that's exactly what they were. Tiny wooden sticks, which could have been mistaken as toothpicks. It didn't look threatening to me, so I didn't get nervous.

I had never felt pain like that in my life. I also didn't realize the sticks would be inserted in me *sideways*. The pain was so great, I passed out. When I came to, I heard the nurses yelling at each other in Spanish, in a panic.

"You scared us," one of them told me as I sipped on a boxed apple juice. "Your face was as white as this sheet."

I went home that day, and the pain was so bad, I was hunched over screaming. Jay lay next to me in my bed. I'd be getting my abortion the next day, so I stayed away from any kind of my usual drugs.

The pain eventually got so bad, I called the clinic. They told me not to take anything, since I was going into surgery the next day, but I couldn't sleep. Somewhere in my pain and druggy logic, I decided it would be okay to take a Xanax to finally get some sleep.

Jay took me back to the clinic the next day. Seeing the physical pain I was experiencing, they rushed me through. When I woke up, I threw up all over myself. I was still in pain, but not nearly as much as when the sticks had been in me.

Because he had to go to work, Jay had called Eddie to come pick me up. Still groggy from the anesthesia, it took me a second to realize someone was in the backseat when I got into his car.

"What the fuck is Eug doing here?"

"We were playing poker, and I asked if he wanted to come with me to come get you."

I turned around to look at Eug.

"I didn't know where we were picking you up from," he sheepishly said, avoiding eye contact.

As we drove back home, my pain got worse. I could feel the blood coming out of me, soaking the pad they had given me to wear on my underwear. When I got out of the car, there was a pool of blood in the passenger's seat. Eug looked at me in horror.

"I gotta go pick up some money," Eddie said as he drove off. Eug decided to stay with me. We ordered food, smoked weed, and watched TV as I spent the rest of the day changing the bloody towels on the bed.

I feel like that was my first step to getting off the Oxys.

October 22

My ass hurts. The cheeks, not the hole. (Legs day at the gym.)

October 23

I heard a funny story while getting my blood drawn for my monthly STD test. Apparently some guy went in a week ago, looking to get into the industry. He had obviously never taken an STD test before, because when he came out of the bath-room, his urine cup was filled with semen.

HA-HA!

It reminded me of a story Ivan told me a few years ago. He was shooting a girl's first anal scene, and when he handed her an enema to clean her butt out, she opened the cap right there on the spot, in front of everyone, and drank the solution.

October 27

I did a scene with a BBW today. That means Big Beautiful Woman; basically a fat girl. It was my first time, and it was amazing. There was so much to grab, I got so into it. We fucked all over the place, and even after the cameras were off I kept eating her pussy. She smelled a little different from other girls. I liked it. Plus, it made me feel really skinny.

October 28

Last night I had that dream again where I'm cheating on my diet. I kept saying, "I shouldn't, or should I?" as I ate every pastry in sight.

Needless to say, I woke up feeling horrible.

I think I'll go to yoga to clear this negative energy before today's orgy scene. I wanna go in with a positive attitude.

November 1

Went to the nail place the other day with Mia and her sister. A fan recognized me from outside the shop and came in. He offered to pay for my manicure. I laughed it off and told him no, thank you very much for the offer, but I couldn't possibly, and then remembered Mia and her sister.

I half joked, "I'll take you up on your offer if you pay for my friends, too."

The gentleman declined and left. But ten minutes later, he came back with a note in his hand. "I changed my mind. I'll pay for all your manicures."

He paid, gave me the note, shook all of our hands, and left.

We high-fived as we left the shop and congratulated ourselves on scoring free manicures, and I read the note aloud in the car. It included his phone number and email address.

That was two weeks ago, and now I need another manicure. But I'm scared to go back by myself. I think I'll just try a new spot.

November 3

Was bored on set today and had the random urge to see if the domain "hooker.com" was taken. It was. I thought I was being funny, but when it loaded on my phone, the first picture to pop up was me on my knees with cum all over my face. Talk about a reality check.

November 12

Yesterday while Toni was on set, I looked at his Twitter. He posted a picture of himself with Renee, and they were on a massage table.

"You got a massage today, lucky," I texted him.

"No. I gave the massage." He corrected me.

"Ooohhh."

"You massaged too, right? I saw your Instagram," he asked.

"No. I was a doctor." I corrected him.

Being in a porno couple is funny.

November 13

I just saw the commercial for a romantic comedy starring Meryl Streep and Tommy Lee Jones and nearly vomited. Nothing but respect for Meryl Streep, but old people falling in love is just gross.

November 14

Saw a psychic for a show on BBC today. She said I wouldn't win any AVN Awards this year. What the fuck . . .

November 21

When I was younger, my grandmother (RIP) used to tell me about the time she cracked a raw egg open and inside was a dead chicken fetus.

Someone told me today that the eggs we eat aren't fertilized.

Until this moment, every time I cracked an egg open, I had a split second of fear that an egg miscarriage would come falling out of the shell.

I feel like my whole life has been a huge lie.

Also: Am I crazy, or is it weird that vegetarians eat eggs? It's kind of abortion-ish.

November 28

Hearing my thirty-seven-year-old boyfriend play video games upstairs while talking shit into an earpiece is something I never thought would happen to me.

November 29

I was masturbating this morning and my fucking leg kept cramping right as I was about to cum. I swear this happened like eight times in a row before I just decided "fuck it" and gave up. Whenever this happens, I feel like God is punishing me for being a whore.

I wonder if this ever happens to dudes? Like how funny would it be if it happened to a male performer, during a scene?

On top of everything else, it's fucking raining outside and I need to get groceries. Sometimes I think life would be easier if I just committed a crime and got on house arrest.

December 8

At yesterday's shoot, I used kegel balls for the first time. I put them in my pussy while Derrick fucked my asshole. It felt really good. I like them so much, the director let me keep them. She said they're actually all the rage with women right now; apparently if you keep them in your pussy while you run your errands, your pussy muscles will get stronger.

I have them in now, and I'm gonna keep them in when I go to boot camp later. This is gonna be either fucking awesome, or the worst idea ever.

Update:
I chickened out and didn't wear the kegel balls to boot camp. It would've been too embarrassing if they came rolling out.

December 15

While I was running on the treadmill today, my trainer told me, "Marathon runners have average bodies." I think I've met my body dysmorphic match.

Also, running on the treadmill next to me was a MILF with two black eyes from a recent nose job surgery. It felt very L.A.

December 17

Interesting conversation with Mia today. She told me she was dying to know what it was like to fuck with a penis. I told her I was dying to know what it felt like to get fucked in the ass if I had a prostate. We promised if we wake up tomorrow as men, she'll use her penis to fuck my prostate-filled ass.

December 18

Woke up this morning to an email from Groupon.
"European Facials for $50."
I had barely enough time to get excited before I realized what they actually meant. Euro men are the best.

December 20

Did a TV show today to promote Fleshlight, the "Number One Selling Male Sex Toy in the World."

It went like this:

Host: "You girls all have your signature textures. Why don't you tell me more about that?"

Stoya: "Mine's the Destroya. 'Cause my name. Like Stoya. It has teeth. But they're really soft, gummy teeth that feel amazing."

Misty: "Mine is Bump & Grind. 'Cause you gotta feel that bump, and that grind, baby."

Kayden: "They named mine the bookworm. My fans know me as just that, and the pattern resembles a worm." She's the perfect fucking package. Blond, skinny, gorgeous, smart, and funny.

Me: "My texture is the Dragon. Because I'm Asian."

Oh, also, I bought Toni a Mercedes for Christmas this morning. Hope I don't regret it.

December 22

Back in NYC since yesterday, except I'm in fucking Flushing, Queens, until tomorrow for a dancing gig. Toni's gonna fly in tomorrow morning and then we'll head to my parents in Brooklyn for the holidays.

During my first show last night, I danced to the Weekends' "Wicked Games" and I overheard a drunk wiggerish white boy yelling, "Yo, this is the best song I've ever heard!" over and over to his other wiggerish friend. It was hilarious.

Also hilarious, there was a sign in the locker room which read:

"Tops must be taken OFF at the end of the 2nd song when you're on STAGE.

"Anyone who 'forgets' will be sent home and/or suspended."
I took a picture of it. Maybe I'll start a coffee table book.

December 25

Toni proposed last night!
We had breakfast with my parents, and I guess they knew the whole time . . . Toni talked to them the night before. He did it by the big tree at Rockefeller Center. My ring is fucking gorgeous. AGHH!!! I'm engaged! My mom cried.

December 27

Saw my cousin's baby last night.
I want one I want one I want one.
Maybe next year.
Heading back home to L.A. tomorrow.

January 1

We got married by Elvis on the thirtieth. We got back to L.A. and decided "Fuck it, let's just go to Vegas now." It was fucking perfect and very *True Romance*-y. Our Elvis cut his chin shaving and had a spot of blood that I couldn't stop staring at throughout the whole ceremony. I kept thinking, *AIDS*. I told Toni after and he said he stared at it the whole time, too.
It's kind of cool to be able to say, "I got married last year," even though it was only a few days ago. Ha-ha.

January 3

I turned twenty-eight today. I also realized I've been on Facebook for seven years. That's longer than I've done anything.

I think I'm getting the flu. I feel like shit. Or maybe it's just the thought of getting closer to thirty and not being sure what I will do with the rest of my life when I'm too old to shoot porn.

January 5

Definitely have the flu, had to cancel all my upcoming shoots. I did an interview this morning over the phone, though, where I was asked what my most memorable sexual encounter was.

I thought about it for a second, and realized my most memorable sexual experience is a little gay. Not gay as in two people of the same sex banging, but gay like unicorns and rainbows.

It was last year in Cabo. Toni and I were vacationing at an all-inclusive resort, the kind where you pay one flat fee upon arrival, and everything for the rest of your stay is free—meals, drinks, suite, activities . . . did I mention drinks?

On our first night there, we were walking along the beach holding hands (see what I mean by gay?) when we came across a roasting fire. No other people were in sight. I barely had enough time to process that this was a once-in-a-lifetime opportunity to have sex on the beach, by a fire no less, before Toni pushed me down and threw himself on top of me. He lifted my dress, pushed my panties to the side, spit on his hand to lubricate his hard cock, and shoved it inside me. I moaned loudly; we were in public, but like I said, there was no one in sight. Besides, I wasn't going to waste this moment and have silent sex. It feels better when it's loud, and that's a fact. He made me cum, and when he felt my pussy throb, it made him even harder.

"Cum in my pussy, I need your cum," I told him.

I clenched my pussy and worked on building my own orgasm to match his.

As he came, I swear to fucking God I saw a shooting star. And then I came one final time.

That magical moment where I saw a shooting star as the man I love came inside of me was definitely my most memorable sexual experience.

Anyways, I ended up telling them about the time I got gangbanged by seven dudes.

January 10

Finally over the fucking flu. Finally shaved my pussy today. As I showered, I was horrified at the state of my bush; I can't believe I let Toni fuck me like that. A good measure of love in a relationship is how often she shaves her pussy . . . I'll never let it happen again.

January 11

Had to mail something out for the first time in my life today. I got to the post office before realizing I had no idea how to send out mail. I stood in line and had the lady behind the counter just figure everything out for me. She looked at me like, "What's your excuse?"

I hope she didn't fuck it up on purpose. I know how to gracefully handle eleven dicks at once, but I don't know how to send out mail.

January 15

Heading to Vegas tonight for AVN. I hate packing. I can't wait to eat a big fat burger when it's all done.

January 21

Finally back from Vegas. AVN was successful, I won six awards, including Performer of the Year! Yayy! Celebrated that night with a huge burger from room service. Gonna order pizza tonight, hehe. So excited.

January 27

A little late, but better late than never.
Goals:
1) Quit smoking for real.
2) No more pizza. Only once every two weeks, tops.
3) Write a book.
4) Run faster than the MILFs at boot camp.

15
The Other End of the Stick

I texted Dee.

I'm flaking : (

I'm directing a gangbang movie and the main girl can only do it the same day as the reunion.

Saturday, May 3 was supposed to be the day that only comes but once in a lifetime—the highly anticipated (!) ten-year highschool reunion. It just had to coincide with my directorial debut.

I didn't think I'd care. I didn't even graduate from that school. But for certain, out of the three highschools I had attended, it was the only one that would be holding such a ceremony.

Did I even have fond memories of that school? Stealing our moms' prescription pills to crush, then snort in the bathroom. Inhaling Dust-Off in the hallway before entering class. Calling in to the school secretary as each other's parents to take a "sick" day. It seemed like all the best memories were of escaping the reality of the place.

I told Dee to make sure to text me any good gossip—who's gay, who's rich, who's broke, who's fat, who's on drugs, who's dead.

Then I realized . . . Me. I'm probably the gossip. Guess who's in porn.

A week later, when I directed the first scene of my first movie, right away I started to appreciate being a performer. So much went into a single production that I had never realized. As a performer, I got to set, sat in the makeup chair for an hour and a half, gossiped with the crew and talent, shot some photos, had mind-blowing sex, and went home. As a director—the production started not on the day of the actual shoot, but days, if not weeks, earlier. And I didn't even get laid.

Step one was to book the talent. Most girls in the industry have agents. Some of the guys do, too, but for the most part, they book themselves. There are six major agencies in the business, to go-tos. Generally, to be successful in the business, a girl needs to be signed with one of these agencies. On a typical agency website, a girl will have six to ten photos in various stages of nudity, a list of stats like age, ethnicity, height, and weight, and then another list that lists the sexual acts she offers.

When I first joined the business, I was with an agency called GoldStar Modeling, who at the time was one of the biggest agencies. Running GoldStar was Joel, who was a male performer himself. I remember he made me cry once.

"I'm not comfortable doing bachelor parties—I told you," I said for the umpteenth time.

"It's easy, you just go there, dance for a bunch of drunk guys, get paid, and leave. What's the big deal? You can do porn, but not that? Come on." Joel mocked me.

I've always been easily flustered when pressured, and started crying. "I don't want to do it and you can't make me," I argued like a child.

Ultimately, I didn't do the gig, but I was under contract with GoldStar for two years before I was finally free to leave and join the Spiegler Girls.

The thing about porn talent agencies is that they will all get you work. Especially when you are new. Every director looks at every agency website, and new girls are always going to get booked—everyone wants to see a new girl. The key to a good agency is that they will *continue* to get you work over the course of your career. That's Spiegler. He's the best, and everyone knows it.

Once the talent is booked, it's time to find a location. There are several websites that list shooting locations, but many of the locations are mansions booked directly through the homeowner. I always love seeing houses I've shot in, used in mainstream productions—I'll recognize a house in a TV show that I regularly have anal sex in, or a rapper lip-syncing on a sofa I recently squirted on. The best locations have lots of windows with natural light coming in—that way, the penetration is always well lit and looks beautiful.

After that, it's the boring stuff like getting insurance for the production, hiring one of the makeup artists requested by the performer, preparing the model releases and necessary paperwork for everyone to fill out on set, sending out call-times, and wardrobe requests. On a Gonzo production, the girl usually wears her own clothing. She brings a suitcase full of lingerie, bikinis, and dresses, and together with the director, a decision on the outfit is made.

I'm always interested to see what a girl's porno suitcase looks like—how she packs it, whether it's messy, how much of it is used versus new. I think a girl's suitcase says a lot about her. Some girls throw everything into the suitcase in a tangled mess, with no order whatsoever, the bottoms of their dirty high heels touching the part of their panties that covers the pussy lips. Some girls put all the bras in one bag, and panties in another. I've seen a girl who puts everything on a hanger, including bikinis, and then puts all of it into her suitcase.

Personally, I have a lingerie/bikini-only suitcase, which stays permanently in the trunk of my car. I stuff every lingerie/bikini set in its own individual Ziploc bag, so that I don't misplace anything. I keep a separate duffel bag for shoes only, which stays in my car permanently as well. Everything else, like dresses, schoolgirl outfits, etc., I pack for each individual shoot.

On the day that was supposed to be my highschool reunion, I shot Alexis. Blond hair and huge tits, a person would never guess she was a New York City native, like me.

"You must stick out so much in the city," I always tell her. New York isn't like Los Angeles; people aren't blond, much less with injected lips, and breast/ass implants. Alexis just laughs at this statement and agrees. I think she secretly likes the flashiness of her look. I think I do, too.

Upon opening her suitcase, I noticed Alexis didn't really pack in an organized matter—there was no apparent plan— but it wasn't all tangled up in a giant mess, either. Most of her stuff was new, with the tags still on them. I mentally noted to myself to go lingerie shopping as soon as possible.

We chose for her a tight red dress, with nothing underneath. She would be shooting her first-ever gangbang today, and the setting was a sex club; I figured if I were to ever go to a sex club, I would go sans underwear. So commando it was.

"We're gonna start downstairs with the gloryhole," I told Alexis as she sat in the makeup chair. "Suck the cock for like literally one minute, then we're gonna go into another room, where you'll blow Danny for literally one minute, then walk down a hallway, have sex with John for another minute, then he's gonna grab you by your hair and bring you to the gang-bang room. It'll all be one continuous shot, and that'll be the intro. Once we're in the gangbang room, we'll cut, get all the boys together and hard, and gangbang with no cuts unless we have to."

"I'm so excited!" Alexis exclaimed with her eyes closed as her eyelash glue dried.

"I'm kind of jealous!" I admitted in return. Thinking back to my own first gangbang, I remembered I had stated in several interviews it had been the best day of my life. My boyfriend at the time saw one of them, and consequently broke up with me over it.

"Are you still seeing that guy?" I asked Alexis.

"Who? The last guy? In Queens?" Alexis was a New York native like me.

"Yah, last time I saw you, you were with a guy who's not in the business."

"Oh, I'm done with him. I'm just trying to be single and do *me* for now, you know?"

I did know. Having been through a few relationships over the course of my porn career myself, I was fully aware of how rough it was to maintain one. It's hard to say which is harder—dating someone within the business, or someone outside of it, a "civilian." Both have their pros and cons. The perks of dating someone who works in porn are obvious: They understand the difference between work sex and home sex. When you do a hardcore double penetration scene in the afternoon, they understand you might be too sore to have sex that night. And, on those rare occasions you catch chlamydia or gonorrhea . . . there's no embarrassment when you have to go get medicated together. That's a tough one, when dating a civilian.

"Ummm, hey. I don't know how to say this, but . . . I have chlamydia. Meaning you probably do, too. So . . . can you come with me to the doctor tomorrow so we can get our pills?"

It's an awkward conversation that would most likely never happen in any other situation.

However, dating a porn guy isn't exactly easy, either. The guys you work with every day, those are his friends. Those are the guys he goes out with on Saturday night, the guys he turns to with all of his problems when you two are fighting. If they're not his friends, he's constantly running into them anyway on sets and at the gym. And sometimes, you are even having sex with guys he really fucking hates. For the most part, most of them can keep an objective mind about it—but everyone has bad days.

A civilian doesn't deal with any of this—he is completely on the outside, oblivious to the details of who you are fucking.

The boys started arriving one by one while we shot a little striptease sequence to go in the beginning of the intro. There were seven of them in total. I requested the night before that they all bring a white wifebeater and blue jeans as their wardrobe. Every one of them wore their sex outfit to set, which made me envious; changing in and out of wardrobe was my least favorite part of porn. If I could roll out of bed, hop in the shower, put on an outfit, and stay in that outfit the whole day—only to take it off during sex—my job would be completely perfect.

Once we shot the intro, we took a break. Everyone smoked their last cigarettes, baby-wiped their balls, and did whatever they needed to get their dicks hard.

What followed was a perfect gangbang scene. Alexis started on her knees, crawling down the line of hard cocks, stopping to give each one some alone time with her mouth. At the end of the line, she climbed on top of Prince, sitting on his dick to ride him. Almost as if on cue, the other guys came swarming around the action, throwing their hands in to touch whatever they could: a tit, her face, her clit, whatever. We only cut once. She stayed airtight for about three-quarters of the scene, meaning she had all three of her holes—her mouth, pussy, and ass—filled. At the end, she took two loads in her pussy, and the rest on her face and mouth.

I was jealous. I went home wondering if directing porn was even right for me. It seemed like the shitty end of the stick—more work, less pay, and I didn't even get to orgasm at the end of it. While shooting, I found myself resenting the fact I wasn't in front of the camera. That should have been *me* getting double-penetrated while being choked out. That should have been *me* at the center of attention of all the guys, begging for them to call me a slut.

And I missed my highschool reunion for it.

The next day, I went in to sit with the editor to start on postproduction of the scene. As I put the intro together, and started to see my vision come alive—a girl's journey through a seedy sex club, performing different sexual acts in different private rooms, until ultimately entering the gangbang room, where seven guys were waiting to fuck the shit out of her—I got turned on, in a way I hadn't before. I had put all of this together. It was gratifying, seeing Alexis like that, the look of such ecstasy on her face—all in a scenario I had envisioned. It was real now, right in front of my eyes, on the computer screen. Soon people all over the world would be jerking off to the inside of my brain. It was pretty cool.

Needless to say, when I got home from shooting the second scene a few days later, I felt differently. I felt happy, satisfied, and excited for my future as a director. When Dee texted me, asking how my shoot went, I told her it had been worth missing our reunion. And I meant it.

A Breakup Letter

August 9, 2013

I should state right away that this is a breakup letter. For the last six beautiful years, you've taken care of me. You've watched me grow up, really. When you met me, I was just a young girl who didn't know much. I'm a woman now. You taught me so much about love, life, sex, and myself.

What I mean is, it's not you, it's me.

It just feels lately like . . . I'm outgrowing you. We both knew when we got together, that this wouldn't last forever. Yet somehow, around year two or three of this magical relationship, I managed to make myself forget that. You made that easy, with your wild and reckless ways. I got wrapped up in the thrill of the relationship, the excitement of it all. You were always so good at exciting me. Remember the time I first took it in the butt for you? I was so nervous! I hadn't done it much before you, and you were a perfect gentleman about it. You let me do it at my own pace, in my own way.

Who knew what was to come after that! I certainly didn't expect all of this success. You made this all possible for me.

Or, remember the time in that helicopter . . . ? Or the time with the ten guys in the movie theater? Those are such fond memories . . . from times when the end felt so far away.

You taught me to love myself for who I am. You taught me never to compromise what I want. Whenever people claimed "Gonzo porn lacks depth," I defended you—I showed the world a girl can enjoy herself being fucked like a dirty slut, with no scenario, no context, just straight-up hardcore fucking. You taught me to embrace this side of myself; to let go of the shame that comes along with loving sex. And if it weren't for you, I wouldn't even know how to make my asshole gape in a perfect circle.

So . . . before you find out from someone else, I want you to hear it from me.

I've met someone.

Now, before you get upset . . . Do you remember when I first came to you, it wasn't you I wanted? Do you remember, I wanted so badly to be a contract girl? I didn't even know what you were . . . I didn't even know what "Gonzo" meant.

Well, it's finally happening. With this new offer, I was reminded of my original dream. To be glamorous. To make porn that's beautiful. I also saw a way for me to extend my career . . . to continue living out my dream of turning people on, having sex in front of the camera . . . without putting on a freak show. Without fisting my asshole on a weekly basis. Don't get me wrong: I loved doing those things with you. I wouldn't trade those experiences for anything. But you had to know that phase of my life wouldn't last forever, that my tastes would eventually mature. It's only a matter of time before people are sick of watching me "take it to the next level." Not to mention, before there is no next level.

In feature porn, I'm going to make different kinds of movies. I'm gonna show the world a different side of myself. I'm gonna show everyone I can be just as sexy without putting on a circus show. It's gonna be a new era—I want to make movies that the average woman would want to watch, that couples can watch together. Just as I defended you when people said, "Gonzo has no depth," I want to show that feature porn is still passionate, that I can turn the world on just as much without getting fucked by two cocks in my ass at the same time. I'm gonna learn the fuck out of how to be a good actress, and just you watch, I'm gonna get that AVN Best Actress award. I know you think I can't win anything without you—a part of me was scared of that, too. But you'll see. Like I said, you're the one who taught me to believe in myself.

I know this is confusing because of what I said. I always prided myself as a Gonzo girl, a girl who gave a filthy, hardcore scene every time.

"Gonzo is where my heart is," I'd tell everyone.

And it was. But like I said, I'm in a different place in my life now.

It's time.

Today, I signed a contract to perform exclusively for the top feature porn company in the world—Wicked Pictures. I'm proud and excited to go on this new journey.

You've been so good to me, Gonzo, but I hope you can be happy for me in this next chapter in my life.

I'll always love you, and I hope we can remain friends.

Love, Asa

Haiku

Shaving the butt-hole;

Only thing more im-por-tant

Than shaving the vag.

16
Food Porn

I placed the order online quickly, before the shame could settle in.

"Tell me I have to do it. If you don't, I won't be able to press the button," I told Toni.

"You have to do it. Or I'm leaving you."

"Say it like you mean it. Please, I'm serious—I can't hit the order button."

"Listen, you fucking bitch, I don't care what you eat but order me my fucking pizza before I smack your slutty little face and leave you crying in your closet."

Order sent.

A good amount of my life is spent thinking about food. I'd say 80 percent of my waking hours is a fair estimate. The lack of it, the hunger for it, the fantasy of it, the decision to consume it, the resulting guilt of doing so. I've never been able to understand people who don't eat when they're under stress. Because I'm a class-A emotional eater myself, everything makes me hungry. Being sad makes me hungry. Being happy makes me hungry. Celebration, mourning, avoidance, boredom—they all call for a feast. I can even down a huge meal on Adderall.

Inside, I am an obese woman with the munchies dying to come out. In true game-recognize-game fashion, I can see this handicap in other women who share my pain.

"She wants to be fat so bad," I'll comment, watching a girl eat a salad at a restaurant, as her boyfriend digs into his plate of pasta. "Look how hungry she is," I project.

As I hit the "refresh" button over and over on my inbox, waiting for the confirmation email, I could feel my heart rate rising.

Asalotapuss:

Thank you for placing your Papa John's pizza order via our Online Ordering service. Please find below the details of your order:

ORDER DETAILS

1 Large Original Crust Grilled Chicken Club Pizza (Onions, Bacon, Grilled Chicken, Roma Tomatoes, Mushrooms)

1 Buy any Large Pizza for $11 and get any Second Large Pizza for $9.99

Large Thin Crust with Pineapple

Large Thin Crust Spinach Alfredo Pizza

1 Large Original Crust Steak and Cheese Pizza

1 15 piece Chicken Poppers

1 Add a 2-Liter to your Order

2-Liter Pepsi Max

Delivery Fee $2.99

Grand Total $59.11

Order Type: Delivery

Method of Payment: CASH

Estimated Ready Time: 45–55 minutes

Thank you for choosing to order online with Papa John's Pizza.

That email. My favorite email.

"Are you excited? Are you?" I nervously asked Toni.

"Yes, super-excited to the maximum," he said, comforting me, smiling. He knew the rules to keeping me calm and neurosis free during a cheat session: Show enthusiasm, don't be a Debbie Downer. I needed to know he loved my cheat days as much as I did. "How much time does it say?"

"Forty-five to fifty-five minutes. Not bad. I'll start the timer now." I picked up my phone to do just that.

I went to turn on the TV and automatically pressed the numbers on the remote control for the Food Network. *Paula's Party*, starring Paula Deen, was on.

Perfect.

As Paula deep-fried cupcakes in the background, I asked Toni to tell me what kind of pizza he had ordered. Having placed the order myself, I already knew, but I wanted to hear the words.

"An original crust pizza with mushrooms, bacon, sausage, grilled chicken, and tomatoes. Did you add onions for me?"

I nodded as I envisioned each ingredient on his pizza cooking in the oven. The cheese melting and bubbling, the tomatoes browning ever so slightly, the oils from the meats seeping on to the rest of the pie, floating and glistening. I thought about my own order, a large thin crust with pineapple, in addition to a large thin crust spinach Alfredo pie. I would alternate slices, going back and forth between the sweetness of the pineapple and the savory, salty richness of the Alfredo. That was my favorite, having a variety. And a good quantity of it, too.

It had been two weeks since my last cheat day. The ideal amount of time between cheats was a month, but I would

still enjoy this meal; there were pizza days that were completely undeserved, only days apart from each other. Without
a doubt, the hardest day to avoid eating unhealthy is the day
after I eat pizza. It's like I ingested a drug, it's escaping my
system, and my body is craving more.

Growing up, I was always skinny. I was that girl who could
eat anything and wake up the next morning with a flat stomach. If anything, I was embarrassed about my low weight; I
would lie and say I was one hundred, when I was really about
five to ten pounds short of that.

"Telling a skinny person they're too skinny is like telling
a fat person they need to lose weight," I would foolishly
say.

I wish I could go back in time and smack the shit out of
myself. And then enjoy a huge meal and wake up the next
day with a flat stomach.

Around the end of highschool, I started to gain weight. I
was happy to see my ass filling in, to have Puerto Rican and
black guys whistling at me on the street, yelling, "Damn, look
at that ass on that Asian chick!"

It was when I was living in Tampa that I really started
to pack on the excess weight. Working on the radio show
twice a week, shooting for my website once a week, I spent
the other four days shopping and eating. Keep in mind, this
was Tampa—the healthiest thing around was a processed-
chicken salad with candy-coated walnuts and a corn-syrup-
based dressing from Applebee's. Making fun of my increasing
weight became a common theme on the air.

"You came here as a hot Asian, and now we're stuck with
a Samoan," they'd joke.

It still didn't bother me; I thought it was sexy.

And then I moved to L.A. And I was never happy with my weight again.

It might be that the average woman is thinner in L.A. It might be that my tastes have changed. It might be that porn has made me more self-conscious, or maybe even it's an age thing. The weight I want to be now, I would have cringed at back when I was living in New York.

It's an everyday struggle. Truly it is. I wake up feeling good. I down a smoothie and get myself to the gym, yoga, boot camp, or whatever class I take on that particular day of the week. I take no days off. I get home, eat something light and healthy, and head to my shoot.

So far, so good.

Then, I'm on set and there is junk food everywhere. Once I'm shooting, I'm fine—but before that, as I go through the makeup chair, wardrobe, and dialogue, I am secretly thinking about the bowl of mini chocolate bars and platter of subway sandwiches the whole time. I mean, the entire time. Through conversations with the director, reading my script and memorizing my dialogue, douching my vagina to prepare it for the scene, in the back of my mind, I am always thinking about the food I could so easily just go and eat. Walking by the kitchen one too many times is dangerous.

Once I'm done shooting and I get home, the remainder of the time is spent fighting the urge to say "Fuck it all" and eat a huge amount of empty calories. Fighting the urge to order pizza, go get cheesecake, a burrito, go out for steak.

"Just do it, just enjoy your life," the binge-eating fat kid on my shoulder whispers.

"You can't, you have a shoot tomorrow, the other girls are skinnier than you," the self-loathing anorexic bitch on my other shoulder argues.

My body naturally wants to be twenty-five pounds heavier than it currently is. I've tried every diet under the sun short of bulimia, and that's only due to my lack of a gag reflex. It's proved beneficial to me in my profession, but if I could make myself throw up . . . my whole life would be different. Currently, I was eating nothing but salads (no dressing!) and smoothies. Basically just raw vegetables and fruits.

Except, of course, for cheat days. The days that I lived for.

I looked at the timer. Only ten minutes had passed. Thirty-five to forty-five more to go.

"Let's play a game," I told Toni.

He knew what was up. "Okay. If you could only eat one food for the rest of your life, what would you choose?"

"Aw, that's boring; you already know I'd pick pizza. Or potatoes. You can prepare them so many ways. Mashed, baked, au gratin . . ."

"Okay. What's my favorite food?"

I thought about it. He liked so many things. "The Spanish sausages with tomato bread and cheese!" I screamed. "Oh! And soup!" I added. "Another! Another game!"

"It's your last day on earth. You can have any dinner you want. Go."

This was one of my favorites. "I'd start with lobster bisque—"

"No salad?" Toni joked.

"Fuck a salad, it's my last day on earth. If only I never had to eat another fucking salad again, oh my God . . . Okay, so lobster bisque, hmm. Actually I'd just go to a buffet. And have some of everything. And then red velvet cheesecake for dessert. And then back to the buffet." I could taste the foods as I thought about them. I was so excited for my pizza!

Just as I hit the maximum amount of excitement level for our delivery, I started to realize how I was going to feel tomorrow. It's the worst feeling, the morning after a cheat day—I wake up, remembering the night before, and the real self-hatred begins. I feel sluggish. I feel fat. And I am so far away from my next cheat day.

I closed my eyes and pretended I was just waking up, and I had eaten the pizza last night. Feeling horrible, I wanted to cry.

Should I cancel the order? Was it going to be worth it? I would eat this pizza tonight and pay for it for the next three days, at least—I would feel self-conscious on set in my lingerie, no doubt.

As the two girls on my shoulders argued once again, my phone rang.

"Hi, this is Papa John's. I'm downstairs with your delivery."

Every bit of unsureness disappeared. We both jumped up, and Toni went down to collect our food while I set up the coffee table in front of the TV.

After inhaling my two pies, after Toni gorged on his own pie and chicken poppers, we lay on the sofa, not moving.

"I'm so gross," I whined.

"It's okay, you deserve it. Tomorrow we eat healthy again," Toni assured me.

We cleaned up and went to bed. I lay on my stomach, being too full to lay any other way without gagging. I set up my iPad to read when I felt something on my back. Toni was jerking off, kneeling behind me. I threw my ass in the air and smiled.

And then I really thought about it. I wasn't so sure I felt like having sex. "I'm so fat," I whined again.

Indifferent to it, Toni hovered over my back, stuck his dick in me, and whispered in my ear, "So is my cock." Fucking me hard, but all I could think about was how full my stomach was. Was this what it felt like to be pregnant? Just really, really full, all the time?

As Toni fucked me, forcing my body to move back and forth, my stomach moving up and down, I swore that if this was what pregnant sex felt like, I'd be celibate for nine months.

I felt liquid come up my chest, into my throat, and onto the back of my tongue, where I tasted the throw-up. Just a little.

"I'm gonna throw up," I said.

"Okay, I'll be fast," Toni said with his eyes closed.

And before I had time to even think to myself,

Married sex . . .

he came.

17
Nerves

It was twelve noon, and despite having been up for hours already, I wasn't ready to open the blackout curtains of my hotel room. I had been pacing back and forth across the hotel room, nervous as fuck. The sunlight would have somehow made everything too real. *Back and forth, back and forth.* I was scheduled to host the AVNs that night—the biggest award show in the porn business. Just to be asked to host was an honor, really. I chain-smoked. Why? I didn't smoke anymore. Right now, though, the only thing I could envision doing with my hand was to hold a cigarette in between my first and middle finger, rhythmically, robotically, switching between holding it up to my lips and flicking the ashes on the floor. My mind was racing with one run-on sentence after another. *Back and forth, back and forth.*

"Don't worry, you're going to be great," Toni said with a smile from under the crisp, clean white sheets of the hotel bed. AVN week in Vegas is a big party week for everyone in porn. Except me. Toni was hungover, still in his underwear, hadn't shaved, showered, nothing. How could he? The room was barely light enough to see each other.

"I'm not fucking nervous, I'm just bored," I answered as naturally as I could. I knew the speed of my delivery gave me away. If there's one thing I hate, it's being called out on being anything but cool. "Hand me a cigarette," I said, distracted.

"You're still smoking the one in your hand, Asa." Toni was smirking at this point. He wouldn't admit it, but I could see the outline of his face. He was smirking. "Just relax."

Something about hearing the word relax has the exact opposite effect. "I don't WANT to fucking *relax* right now, Toni! I'm bored as fuck and I'm fucking starving."

"So eat something."

Men can be so cruel.

"I can't! My dress is too tight as it is. Why are you doing this to me? You always do this! Please, just be nice to me!" I yelled.

Toni sighed and turned on the TV. I knew I was being crazy. He knew I knew I was being crazy. The awards were still hours away, though, and it was like the more normal I tried to act, the worse my behavior ended up being.

The truth was, I wasn't nervous about hosting. I wasn't nervous about fitting into my dress.

I was nervous I wouldn't win anything.

As a child, I don't remember being competitive. I was never any good at sports. Having no siblings, I just did my own thing, never expecting to be the best at any particular activity or subject. If anything, I was the opposite; I preferred to stay in the background, going unnoticed.

"Shy people never get anything," my mother would repeatedly tell me in her accented English. I'd nod, understanding, but fully planning on sticking to my timid ways.

Fast-forward to middleschool, when I gave Dan Sherzer my first blowjob. I was the talk of the school. All of a sudden

I was the bad girl. Girls were asking me for boy advice. Boys were asking me on dates. It felt good.

Fast-forward again a few years to highschool. I was arguably the biggest slut in my grade. I hung out with derelicts, the "rebels" of New York private school. We thought we were badasses; we did everything other kids wished they could.

Fast-forward one final time to my fourth year in porn. I had won fourteen AVN awards, I was one of the top three current pornstars, and was regarded as the biggest Asian star in the history of porn. Tonight was the AVN Awards. I was nominated for the coveted Performer of the Year award for the third year in a row, but had yet to win it; I wanted it more than I could ever admit to anyone but myself.

"Give me the fucking remote," I mumbled as I walked toward Toni. I grabbed it out of his hands and switched the television off, then threw the remote on the floor.

That was it for Toni. "I'm going down to meet with Ramon," he calmly said as he got up. He knew that when I acted crazy, it was a losing battle. I'd get as crazy as he'd let me, only to apologize crying when I later came to my senses.

I cried for him to stay, that I was sorry, but it was too late. "I don't want to be alone," I sobbed. But he left.

Alone in the room, I had nothing to do. I didn't want to be in my own company, I couldn't stand myself right now. I started to wonder if Toni knew the real reason I was so nervous. If he did, what did he think of me? He knew I wanted the award, but to this degree? Was it nuts of me to want, no, *need* this superficial thing so badly? For sure, he couldn't possibly think I was mentally stable if something this dumb could hold such great importance for me.

I started to get mad at Toni. It's what happens when I'm disappointed in myself. Conjuring up all the times I was angry with him, I went to throw my cigarette in the toilet. The time he accidentally called me fat. The time he lied to me about the coke he had thrown away, when in fact it was still in his jeans pocket. The time he called me an 8 out of 10.

"Well, first of all, you're not tall enough to be a ten," he explained.

"I'm your girlfriend. You should consider me at the very least an eleven!" I screamed in tears.

Thinking about it was making me angry all over again. Did Toni even realize there were millions of men out there who would give up a finger to be in his position? I lit another cigarette and tried to calm myself down. Why did I need so much reassurance from the outside? Toni, the awards . . . why couldn't I just have enough confidence to not need validation from others? When did I become this insecure mess?

My biggest regret in life is not asking my parents for a brother or a sister. Yes, that was it—that was the root of all my problems. I have the typical only-child complex: needing of space, yet eternally lonely. Selfish and entitled could probably be thrown in there as well. I live in my head more than in reality, and all of my personality flaws are because of my lack of siblings. I hated myself for it.

As I thought about it, the loneliness started to kick in. I texted Toni.

"I'm sorry I'm being crazy. Please come back up. You're right, I'm nervous. I promise I'll be good."

He didn't reply. He knew I wasn't ready.

I put out my cigarette, and before my anger could replace the loneliness, I lay on the bed to masturbate.

I envisioned my usual starters. Toni kissing me, Toni choking me, Toni slipping the tip in, Toni telling me he owns me. It's always been this way; when in a relationship, I only think of my significant other when I touch myself. Without consciously trying, I'm mentally faithful. I started to think about walking into our bedroom and catching Toni fucking another girl. It doesn't matter who she is, or what she looks like. It's the fact that he's fucking another girl, and not giving a fuck about me. I think back to all the porn I've watched with him in it, making other girls squirt, cum, scream.

Over the last year or so, around the same time I decided with conviction to stop dotting my i's, I had developed a new-found dedication to masturbating loudly. First, it started with a little whimper here and there, then over time graduated into moans. Nowadays, I was full out screaming, "I need your cum in me, please!" as I came. It felt better being loud. Often, I wonder if my neighbors think I'm cheating on Toni while he's gone. But *life is too short to masturbate silently*, I'll declare to myself, and scream on. Here, on this hotel bed, was no different. "Toni, please," I moaned as I tensed up my legs. As I let go and came, I screamed—

"It's your ass, you own me!"

As I came down from my orgasm, I heard someone cough in the hallway. I felt a pang of shame. Maybe for being so loud, maybe for masturbating in general. This shame thing, after cumming—was it a forever thing? Would I ever stop feeling guilty after rubbing one out? As a kid, I got caught all the time. There was a period of time my mother wouldn't let me fall asleep with the covers over me, because she knew I would just start rubbing myself. In spite of it, or perhaps because of it, I can't fall asleep now without my hand on my pussy.

I texted Toni again.

"I miss you."

Nothing.

I got dressed and went downstairs to the gym, but got a smoothie instead and walked back up to the room. After attempting to start the book I had just downloaded on Kindle, I purchased a movie on the hotel on demand, but hardly watched it. I was restless.

"I'm pregnant," I texted Toni as I lay in the bed, with my hand on my pussy.

"I don't believe you."

At least he replied.

I quickly googled "positive pregnancy test" on my phone and hit Images. On page three was the perfect photograph, amateur enough but the "positive" outcome clear. I saved it to my phone, sent it to Toni, and waited for a reply.

I'll admit, you're pretty funny.

Finally, two hours of plucking my body hair later, he called me. "When I get there, you better be naked on your fucking knees." He hung up.

I undressed out of the gym clothes I still had on, got on my knees, and waited for him to open the door. When he walked in, I immediately crawled toward his cock. He slapped my face.

"You think you're running the show here? Sit back and close your eyes, you stupid bitch."

I was happy to oblige. I was happy just to see his face, no matter the angry expression in his eyes. I sat back on my feet, eyes closed, and listened to him take his watch off, then his sweater, then his belt, and the rest of his clothes. My heart melted at the scent of him. It's amazing how when you take away one basic sensor, the others kick in twice as strong. I heard him kick off his shoes, as his hand came down on the back of my head, grabbing my hair. He slammed my face into the carpet and dragged my face onto his feet. I opened my mouth and began to worship him with my tongue, starting at the tip of his toe.

"Are you sorry? You little bitch, did you miss me?"

I nodded as best as I could, as he took his bare foot and stepped on my head, lodging my face sideways between his foot and the floor. I could smell where I had ashed my cigarettes earlier.

"Then show me." He took his foot off my head and I kissed my way up his leg. His cock was rock hard. I kissed it all over, every square inch, square centimeter of it.

"I missed you so much. I won't be crazy. I promise I'll be good," I begged as I rubbed the side of my cheek on his dick. It was so hard, I knew he wanted me as much as I wanted him.

"Shut up." Toni grabbed the back of my head and shoved my head down his cock. I gagged, but he was relentless, repeatedly hitting the back of my throat, and going deeper with every shove. My eyes started to water. Upon seeing this, he pinched my nose so that I couldn't breathe. I panicked. I started to hit Toni's leg and waved my own, kicking the floor away. Finally, Toni let me breathe. "Are you going to do as I say? Or be a little bitch?"

Slap!

"I'm gonna do as you say, I swear. I'm gonna be good." With tears streaming down my face, I forced his cock down my throat and waited for him to pinch my nose. This time I didn't dare move.

"Good girl." He bent down to kiss me. I missed his lips so much. This is what I live for.

Faster than I could say "I love you," Toni stood back up, grabbed my hair from the top of my head, and dragged me across the carpeted floor. Scrambling on all four limbs, I tried to catch up with him so that my hair wasn't pulled so hard. In one motion he lifted me up by my hair to stand, and I was leaned up with my face against the wall. He rubbed his cock between my legs. It was so hard, I could almost feel it throbbing on my inner thigh. My pussy was so wet, it felt like I had pissed myself.

I heard him spit, then felt his fingers inside me. He fucked me with his hand and I knew what was coming. I couldn't help it, I wasn't in control. The second he took his hand out, I squirted all over the floor.

"Get down and lick it up." I would do anything to please him, so I got down on the floor and licked the dirty, ash-and-squirt-covered carpet while he watched me, stroking his cock. I wanted it so bad. I knew he would put me through obstacles before letting me have it.

I hate the taste of squirt. As I licked it up, I told myself I deserved this.

When I did this long enough for his liking, Toni directed me to stand up and go to the bed.

I lay down on the bed, on my back. Toni came and lay on top of me.

"You want to know a secret?" he asked.

I nodded.

He smiled for the first time since he walked into the room. "I missed you."

I started to sob. It was what he said. It was how much my head hurt from him pulling my hair, how much my jaw hurt from being slapped too hard. How my face smelled like fucking squirt. It was how bad I had missed him, how much I hated myself for being so insecure. And how happy I was he was here.

As I shook with tears running down my face, he kissed me all over, and whispered how beautiful I was as he finally put his cock inside of me. Immediately the muscles in my pussy grabbed on, and I came almost instantly. I had been waiting for what seemed like an eternity.

He fucked me like this for a while, and made me cum over and over.

"I own you," he told me as he took his dick out. Rubbing it on my ass, he pushed my legs farther back. "Hold your legs there," he gently commanded as he pushed the tip into my other hole. I held my breath while he worked his way in. Gradually, inch by inch, he went farther into my ass. All the way in, the head of his cock hit the perfect spot.

"Only your cock feels this good," I told him like I had told him so many times before. I clenched my ass and concentrated on orgasming. "Please cum in me, I miss your cum, I need it," I begged him. I was at the point of cumming but I waited for him to catch up. "I want to cum so bad but I need to feel your cock throb. I'll keep it in me all day like a good girl."

That did it. As he came into my ass, moaning, squeezing my waist, I let go, too. I could feel the cum coming out of his dick, spreading in my ass.

By the time we were done, it was time for me to go to my makeup artist's room. Toni walked me there and came to pick me up when I was done. We walked the red carpet, and I went on to host the show with absolutely zero mistakes. I won my Performer of the Year award, along with five others. Toni and I went to celebrate at the club after the awards, and we ended the night back in the hotel room, me back to my normal self.

Sometimes a girl just needs the crazy fucked out of her.

Letter to My Future Child

Dear future child of mine,

By the time you read this letter, you may already be old. You may still be young, or you may never get to read this at all. Whatever the case, I hope I will have had the courage to tell you about my life. And I hope you can accept who I was before you were born.

You see, Mommy was a pornstar. Not just any pornstar—she was an award-winning anal queen.

Mommy wanted to be a star all her life, and was lucky enough to be one, even if it was only for a few short years, even if she was only really considered a "star" in certain circles. Maybe you want to be a star one day. Maybe you want to be a doctor. Or a teacher. Maybe you want to grow up and be an artist who takes donations in the subway station just to support their passion/lazy significant other. That's okay, too. Mommy wants you to do whatever you want with your life—because that's what a person is entitled to do.

Did I ever tell you how your father and I met? Have you asked that question yet? I wonder if I told you we met at work. How detailed did I get? Maybe I avoided the truth altogether and told you we met on eHarmony.com. I hope so badly that I told you something close to the truth.

Mommy met Daddy in her first DP scene. Do you know what that is? DP means double penetration. That means during the sex scene, Mommy had one man's penis in her vagina, while she had another man's penis in her asshole, at the same time. The scene wasn't supposed to go that way. Mommy had never even shot an anal scene at that point. But she was falling in love. And when people are falling in love, strange things happen sometimes.

The scene was the first time Mommy ever met Daddy in real life. She had seen Daddy's movies, and was fascinated. She had never seen a man who could dominate a woman that way. He would treat a woman like a filthy whore one minute, choking her to the point of passing out; and then slap her across the face the next minute, to regain consciousness, so she would awaken to him making love to her, whispering sweet nothings in her ear. Mommy was determined to meet Daddy.

Daddy had seen Mommy's movies, too, and he was a fan. But Daddy lived in Spain, and only came to work in America once a year. So their paths didn't cross for a long time.

It was July. Daddy was in America. Even now, he always reminds Mommy he came to the country looking for her.

Mommy was shooting a big movie, and requested Daddy come be in it. She wanted him to be in a three-way with her and another boy. Daddy agreed to take the job. They were both so excited, but at the time, neither of them realized the feeling was mutual.

The first moment Mommy saw Daddy, it was something like love. Mommy, being a Capricorn, obviously doesn't believe in silly things like love at first sight; but this was something special for sure. Let's say from the moment she laid eyes on Daddy, she started falling in love. He looked at her so intensely, it made her nervous at the bottom of her chest. He kissed her passionately, something she didn't do so often in her scenes. He and the other boy had sex with her and made her cum over and over. Mommy felt drunk. When Daddy was inside Mommy's vagina, it felt so good—better than any other penis she had ever had inside of her. Which was saying a lot. It hit all of the right spots, and she felt like he could make her do anything. She wanted to submit everything to him. So Mommy begged Daddy to put it inside of her ass. She begged and begged, and he gave it to her. She opened her legs wider, he spit on his hand, rubbed the spit onto her asshole, and put his dick inside, first the tip, then the head, then the whole shaft. He knew she had never shot an anal scene before. He was gentle at first, but as she moaned, he could feel she was opening up. He started to pound harder. Mommy was entranced.

During it all, Mommy had her hand on the other boy's dick. She held on to it like an anchor, as Daddy slid his dick in and out, in and out. Mommy looked up at the boy with pure happiness painted all over her face. The boy knew what needed to happen.

The boy crawled around Mommy, and as Daddy was making love to her ass, slid his own penis into her vagina. The feeling was overwhelming, but in the best way. It was like an awakening. Mommy cupped her hand over her mouth and looked up in ecstasy, above the camera, into the eyes of Sam, the nice lady directing the movie.

"Just keep going, I can cut this out of the movie if you want later. Just keep going." Sam knew Mommy's first DP would be a highly marketable scene to capture. She was Mommy's friend, and didn't want to ruin a perfect moment with anything like logic or sensibility. She knew something magical was happening in Mommy.

Mommy kept going. She never knew such a sensation existed. It was literally the most amazing thing she had ever felt. If ever there was a moment she thought she could die happy, that was it. At the age of twenty-five, she foolishly thought she had seen it all. Maybe you are at an age when you feel this way. But in that second that both penises were in her, everything changed. If something like this was out there, previously undiscovered to her, there had to be so much more still.

Daddy and the other boy DP'd Mommy for a while after that. After they were done, they came huge loads on her face.

Mommy was more infatuated than ever with Daddy. She asked him for his number. They met up a only a few times before Daddy had to go back to Spain again.

The scene went on to win "Best DP scene" at the AVN Award Show that year. Do you know what the AVN Award Show is? It's the most prestigious award show in porn, considered the "Oscars" of the business. The girls even wear long gowns that cover up most of their bodies to the event. See, that's how you know it's serious.

Over the next few years, Mommy and Daddy would only see each other when Daddy came to America.

Mommy was lonely, though, as having sex for money can be a very lonely business, and Daddy had his whole life in Spain; his business, his life, his friends and family. She briefly dated a boy to fill the void in her life. The boy was insecure, crazy, and loved her only in the way someone who hated himself could. He would later come out of the closet and start performing in gay porn, much to Mommy's embarrassment.

Finally, one Valentine's Day, Daddy was shooting a movie in America. He hired Mommy to work with him in it. He gave her a rose while she sat in the makeup chair with a buttplug in. It was all very romantic, obviously. The scene was electric. Mommy asked Daddy to come spend the night. He agreed. From that day forward, they were together every day until he had to leave back to Spain. And when he did leave, Mommy followed him. They went back and forth between the two countries until they got married so Daddy could stay with Mommy in America forever.

So do you see? If Mommy had never exposed her insides to the Internet, she would never have gotten the greatest gift in her life—you.

I hope you can see how happy I am with all the choices I have made in my life, and understand why living my dreams out, no matter what they were, was absolutely critical in creating your life, too. I hope I haven't caused you pain, and if I did, I hope you can forgive me. Lastly,

I hope I will have been the kind of mother who accepted you, and loved you unconditionally, for every bit of greatness that you are.

Love,
Your Mom

18
ONE

I stepped off the bus. It had been a three-hour ride, and I was groggy from the last twenty minutes, in which I had finally been able to fall asleep. Looking around, I didn't see Travis or Gina. It was cold as fuck, even colder than the city. Gray, empty, and quiet, this was definitely smack in the middle of bumblefuck nowhere. One single doughnut shop, a parking lot, and nothing else in sight. The only noise was the wind, and the occasional car that drove by. It struck me as the kind of place that might produce a lot of guys named Don. Hardly anyone had gotten off at this stop with me.

As I decided to sit down on the bench, Travis came walking up to me. I had only met him a few times, but he was easy to spot: bleached blond hair, and dressed in what I would later come to recognize as the typical porn-guy attire: affliction shirt, Ed Hardy jeans, tacky men's jewelry.

"Gina's in the car," he said smiling as we walked toward the parking lot. "Are you nervous?"

After thinking about it for a second, I replied, "I don't think so."

As unappealing as it may sound to the majority of the world, I had been fantasizing about putting my sex life on public display for some time now. The same way other women my age were naturally programmed to want a child, I felt porn was something I needed to do. I knew I couldn't be happy if I didn't give it a shot; I knew if I didn't try it, I'd forever look back on my life and regret it.

Back home in the Lower East Side of Manhattan was a boy I was dating, Evan, and our roommates Peter and Stephen, who were boyfriends. I wasn't sure if that would be my home at the end of this day.

"Everyone in porn has herpes" was Evan's main argument.

"It would be worth it" was my stubborn reply.

I got into the backseat and Gina turned around. We chatted about how things had been, what was new—which, for me for the most part, was nothing. Less than a year ago, I had moved back home to New York City from Florida, and I had pretty much been sitting on the sofa since then. Upon moving, I had gotten myself clean of Oxys and cigarettes, which I didn't mention. Gina talked about the awards she and Travis had won at the AVNs a couple of months ago.

When we arrived at the house, the makeup artist was already there. I set my duffel bag down and filled out some paperwork before sitting in his chair. Although I was using my real first name, it was strange, writing down my full porno name for the first time. I looked over my shoulder as I wrote it down, as if at any moment someone would point down at what I had written and tell me, "That's not you."

"How do you want your makeup?" The makeup artist asked as I sat down in front of him. I just shrugged with a smile. I didn't know.

As it turned out, I hated the makeup he put on me. My own reflection frightened me as I walked into the bathroom.

I quickly went to get my own makeup bag and fixed it to my liking. Today, of all days, I wanted to feel like myself.

They dressed me in a blue polka-dotted bikini and I posed on an ottoman in a white room with shag carpeting for my box cover pictures. The photo shoot part I was used to—I had done it so many times already for the radio show and my solo-girl website—I could have done it high as a kite and half asleep. In fact, I had.

The first sex position we did was cowgirl. Up until right now, I had anticipated this moment to be a nervous one. An anxious one. At the very least, I thought I would question my actions for a moment; I had envisioned myself thinking. *Here we go*, taking in a deep breath, and then going for it.

I neither felt nor thought any of those things. What I felt was empowered. Invincible. The whole time, I was conscious of the camera, and the fact that men everywhere would be watching me. It pushed me in a way I had never been pushed; it was a new high, and I knew I was hooked right away. In many ways, it was the best sex I had ever had up until that point in my life.

It was as if I had never really been turned on before. I was always curious, horny, wanting to have sex. This was different. It felt like there was literally a spotlight on me, highlighting my every move, making me feel sexier than I ever had. I thought about people watching me with their friends. Watching me in shame. Watching me while fucking their own partners. Watching me for hours on end, jerking off in front of a computer screen while their significant other slept in oblivion upstairs. As we moved through the positions, I felt certain and confident in what I was doing. I couldn't wait for it to be over, so that I could reminisce every wonderful second.

I never felt so much attention. I never felt so wanted.

Exhausted, I passed out on the bus ride home thinking about what my new life would be like. I would sleep with all the best fuckers in the country. Men all over the world would watch me and jerk off. The first step was done. From here on out, this was what I wanted to do. For the first time ever, I was excited for the rest of my life.

When I woke up, we were already at Port Authority. Stepping off the bus for the second time today, I automatically walked toward the downtown A train heading toward my parents' house. I wouldn't go back to be with Evan tonight—he would just try to talk me out of it, and my mind was already made up. I smiled to myself, thinking, *I'd be such a catch, I swear; if only I didn't have this urge to have sex in front of the world, engrained in my very being.*

Four days later, I flew out to L.A.

And the journey began.

Afterword

I often wonder whether I'm a chronic masturbator. In the day and age where virtually any question can be answered with a quick Internet search, it's frustrating to not have a definitive diagnosis.

> *Definition chronic masturbation*
> *Symptoms chronic masturbation*
> *Chronic masturbator test*
> *How do I know if I'm a chronic masturbator?*

Nothing I type into the search engine bar seems to come up with a satisfactory result. Not even Yahoo Answers has anything for me—their closest link being *I'm a chronic masturbator and I need to stop, help?!*

It's not like I want help. There are times when I'm expected to be somewhere, and I skip steps in getting ready so that I can masturbate a little longer. I'll need to be at that somewhere by a certain time, and I lay in bed as the minutes turn into hours, making myself orgasm over and over, promising the universe "Just one more and I'll be on my way," only to make the same promise five minutes later. As each orgasm passes, I lose the chance to do my hair properly. I tell myself I can wear the same outfit as the day before. Sometimes, I devise an excuse about traffic and just plan on being late altogether. The process is very time-sensitive—I have exactly thirteen seconds after an orgasm to get up and shake it off before I get horny again. Thirteen seconds goes by pretty fast, so it's a pretty demanding act, in terms of will. If procrasturbating were an Olympic sport, I'd be a fucking gold medalist. But like I said, I don't need help—I've designed a system: I get ready an hour ahead of time so that I'm free to touch myself until the very last second, until I need to get on with my daily schedule. I pack my purse, do my hair and makeup, and get fully dressed (except for pants, which I take out of the drawer and leave at the foot of the bed) before I lie down, close my eyes, and start the cycle.

If not a full-on masturbation addict, I'm certainly an emotional masturbator. When I'm sad, happy, grouchy, or just bored, my hand automatically reaches down into my underwear and onto my clitoris. I can hardly be left alone for a few minutes on a comfortable piece of furniture without rubbing myself. Hotels are the worst—often, the only place to sit down is a bed, so I'm basically just touching myself the entire time I'm in the room.

My first memories of masturbating are from when I was about four or five years old. My mother would often catch me, and proceed to gently scold me. As a result, it's something that's always conjured a feeling of guilt. But it has always been something I could not stop myself from doing. When I saw a pretty girl, or a handsome man on television (hello, Uncle Jesse), I would sneak away someplace I could lie down on my stomach and hump my hand. I even remember there being a period of time I was not allowed to go to sleep with the covers over me, because my mother knew once I was under those blankets, I'd start humping away. Being so young, I wouldn't orgasm, and I didn't even know what sex was—but I knew the feeling of being horny, and I knew touching myself down there felt good. Pregnant women, especially, did it for me—I didn't know how they got pregnant, but looking back, I applaud myself for having the natural instinct that those women *did something* to get themselves that way. I'll forever remember when Maria from Sesame Street got pregnant, and announced it to everyone on the block—those nine months were the golden days of prepubescent masturbation.

Likely because of my mother's attitude towards self-pleasure when I was young, I still sometimes get an over-whelming wave of guilt after I make myself come. It's not every time; it's not even most of the time—I'd say once every hundred times I touch myself. It feels like a cloud of depression just comes over me, and it's impossible to escape—I just ride through it, knowing it will pass soon. It usually only sticks around for ten seconds or so—never more than the thirteen it takes me to get horny again.

Writing this book was a lot like masturbating. Every thought I had, I felt I needed to sit down and type out. My journaling went into overdrive; everything felt important, profound. My porn shoots suffered, as did my daily morning workouts. Not that I lost interest in these things, but once I started writing, I couldn't stop. "Just one more paragraph," I'd tell myself—"I can be thirty minutes late, no big deal."

Every few hundred words or so, I'd read back what I had written, and that familiar wave of self-hatred would come over me. Could I reveal so much? Who was I, to think my life was worth sharing? This writing was total shit—could it even be published? People were only interested in me because I get naked and have sex on camera. Why would they want to know what went on in my mind?

So much self-doubt, so much guilt for oversharing, so much fear of exposing myself, so much shame in the kind of human I was.

But a few minutes would go by and that cloud would once again pass over me, leaving me fiending to share just a little bit more. And, like masturbating, hotel rooms were the worst—I'd feverishly type away all day for hours upon hours until my eyes went blurry. In fact, since writing *Insatiable*, I've become an eyeglass wearer, damaging the 20/20 vision pride I've had my whole life.

Once the book was out, and people had read it, I felt relieved. Much like the way I feel after bringing myself to orgasm, I felt a weight had been lifted off my shoulders. *Insatiable* was received in many ways: Some people loved it. Some were horrified. Some people were deeply offended by it, and some people were thrilled to take a look inside my life. I read every review, every article, every comment below every review and article. I doubt there's a single thing out there said publicly about my book that I haven't read. And although releasing my feelings felt freeing in a way I had never experienced, reading these opinions brought the cloud back. Having been in porn for so many years, I'm used to reading people's views on my body—I'm always too thick, too short, too alien-looking for someone out there. For every ten people who say nice things about the way I'm being anally penetrated, there's one who voices my asshole doesn't gape wide enough for their liking. And that's okay. I understand I'm not everyone's flavor. I look how I look, and there's nothing I can do about it.

My thoughts, however—that's another story. To pour my heart out into a book, to spend a year writing, and rewriting, stories from my real life, only to have them stomped on by someone who didn't approve of my very existence— that hurt. Having lived in a small bubble known as the porn industry for the past six years, I had forgotten how much of the world was not just antiporn, but antisex. People claimed I was delusional for loving my job; some even called me a downright liar. It angered me, after pushing myself to be so truthful, to be dismissed as the complete opposite. In addition, I was called a narcissist, an opportunist, an exploiter. Someone even referred to me as a "chronic disclosure fetishist," a term I had never heard before. These things especially hurt because I knew deep down many were true. I had just never seen them as negative attributes.

I stopped journaling. What was the point? People were just going to knock me down about it anyway. They were right: It was enough that I felt I needed to exploit my body—why did I need to do the same to my brain? Had I no integrity?

The words that hurt the most were those of antisex feminists. I think the main reason I was so ill-prepared for their reactions was that I had not set out to write anything politically correct. The book was something I had written as an extension of my exhibitionistic ways—another way for me to overshare, to feed my inner "chronic disclosure fetishist." I've always considered myself a feminist, and I did not expect to have to defend my book against my fellow sisters. I'm a woman, a human being with common sense—*of course* I'm a feminist! Of course I believe in gender equality! Gender equality includes women being able to do what they want with their sexuality, regardless of what society's viewpoints are—a right that men have had since the beginning of time. While I respect the extremist antisex feminists' personal choice not to make money off of their sexual fantasies, it enrages me that they cannot give me the same respect in return.

While I hate to even admit that these accusations have affected me in any way, it would be dishonest to recount my experience of releasing *Insatiable* without doing so. Over the past few months, my rage has turned into a sense of gratitude—I'm thankful to have a voice, to have a platform to express my feelings on. I may be a porn star, someone who just fucks for money, but I'm also a woman, living life her way, which is important. I've started journaling again; my desire to overshare is back.

So, in addition to shooting porn, that's what I've been up to, between the release of the hardcover and paperback editions of this book. The cloud of negativity is gone, and I'm back to writing nonstop everyday, working on another book. My morning workouts have suffered, my eyes are blurry, hotel stays are once again no longer just about chronic masturbating—and I'm happy about it. I guess my thirteen seconds have passed.

Acknowledgments

First and foremost, Morgan Entrekin, Peter Blackstock, and everyone at Grove Atlantic: Thank you for giving me this chance of a lifetime. I couldn't be more proud to be a part of your roster.

Toni, my husband. Thank you for loving me, putting up with me, and supporting me. Thank you for not snooping through my computer as I wrote this. And if you did, thank you for hiding it so well.

Mark Spiegler, my porn agent and best friend. No amount of words printed on a page could describe my gratitude for your existence.

Dave Choe, my brother/cousin/uncle's wife's grandmother's daughter's niece, twice removed—what are we telling people these days? Thank you for the beautiful cover. You are the best artist in the world.

Last but not least, Marc Gerald—my book agent, aka Literary Suitcase Pimp. Without you, this project would never have even started. Thank you for believing in me, for guiding me, for giving me confidence, and most of all, for inspiring me.

Without you all, this would not have been possible. I thank you from the very bottom of my ~~vagina~~ heart.